CHETNA'S
INDIAN
FEASTS

CHETNA'S
INDIAN
FEASTS

Everyday meals &
easy entertaining

CHETNA MAKAN

love
Chetna x

hamlyn

To Sia and Yuv, with all my love.

First published in Great Britain in 2023 by Hamlyn,
an imprint of Octopus Publishing Group Ltd,
Carmelite House, 50 Victoria Embankment,
London EC4Y 0DZ
www.octopusbooks.co.uk

An Hachette UK Company
www.hachette.co.uk

Distributed in the US by Hachette Book Group,
1290 Avenue of the Americas, 4th and 5th Floors,
New York, NY 10104, USA

Distributed in Canada by Canadian Manda Group,
664 Annette St, Toronto, Ontario, Canada M6S 2C8

ISBN 978-0-600-63767-7

A CIP catalogue record for this book is available from
the British Library.

Printed and bound in China.

10 9 8 7 6 5 4 3 2 1

Editorial Director: Eleanor Maxfield
Art Director: Juliette Norsworthy
Senior Editor: Leanne Bryan
Copy Editor: Salima Hirani
Photographer: Nassima Rothacker
Food Stylist: Rosie Reynolds
Props Stylist: Lauren Miller
Illustrator: Abi Read
Production Manager: Caroline Alberti

Contents

Introduction

If you look up the word 'feast' in the dictionary, you'll find it has a few definitions. A feast is a large meal, typically a celebratory one, for an annual religious celebration, for instance. But you can call a meal at which you eat a lot of good food and enjoy it greatly a feast, too. Also, an elaborate and usually abundant meal, often accompanied by a ceremony or entertainment, can be called a feast. There are other ways to define the word, but for me, it conjures feelings of joy and thoughts of cooking with love for my family and friends to mark any significant occasion or gathering. I find so much joy in planning what to make, in cooking the elaborate meals and in watching everyone savour the food together. Devouring a delicious feast is a marvellous way for people to enjoy one another's company, to enjoy life together. My aim for this book is to pass some of this joy from my kitchen into yours.

Of course, any good feast requires preparation, which, to me, is part of the joy of the event. I find cooking big meals very relaxing. It's like having my own little party in the kitchen before the main party begins. I have definitely inherited this trait. I grew up in a family that loved to cook for and feed people. My parents liked to celebrate both the little and big occasions in life. We always had relatives over for birthdays and festivals, and there were often friends at our table enjoying home-cooked meals with us. Food was always at the centre of these gatherings. Everything was cooked fresh at home and made with love.

I remember clearly that my mum would cook for hours to prepare a feast for everyone without ever breaking a sweat. She would devise the menu first, then gather the ingredients, and she always cooked on the day of the feast itself. She still loves to cook feasts at every opportunity, and often calls me to discuss her menus. I'll then receive wonderful pictures of the feast when everything is served, often showing people enjoying the food.

Like my mum, I believe that food brings people together. It's such a great ice-breaker, as so many people love to talk about it. When I moved to the UK from India two decades ago, I found that food offered a great way of meeting people and getting to know them better. From the colleagues I met in my first job

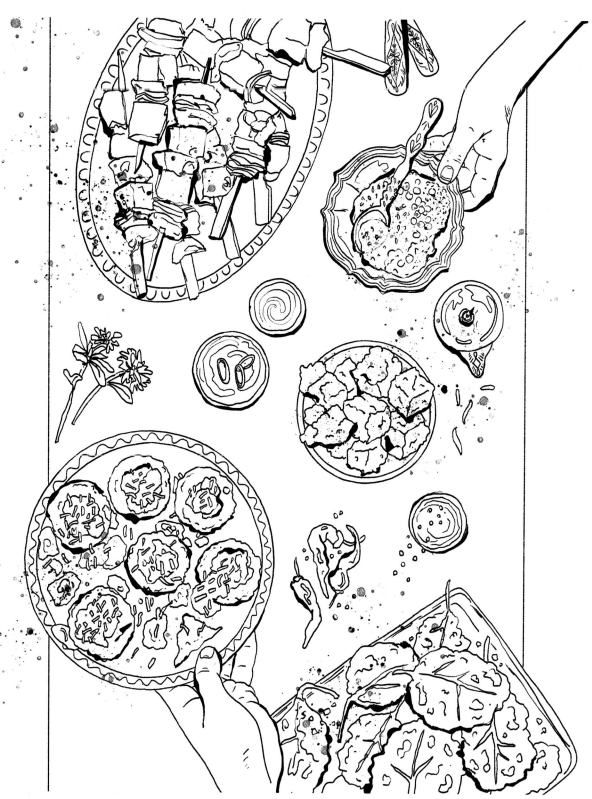

to the lovely mothers I befriended at the toddler play groups, it was discussing or sharing food that seemed to break the ice every time.

We all know how important it is to spend quality time with friends and family, and a delicious feast certainly helps to make any kind of gathering a wonderful event. Each chapter in this book showcases a full menu for a feast designed for a specific type of occasion. These menus contain the recipes that I cook most often for Friday night feasts, picnics, festivals, Sunday brunches and so on. These are the feasts that are loved the most in my own home. I hope you will enjoy them as much as I have enjoyed devising, preparing and devouring them.

I've put a lot of care and thought into creating the menus. Whether you cook one dish or four from a chapter, or go for the full feast, you'll have a wonderful meal. The spices and flavours of each dish in a menu are all balanced in a way that allows you to enjoy them together. There is something for everyone in each menu – vegetable dishes, lentils, chicken and fish, with

a tasty rice dish to accompany, and a bread to scoop it all up. But feel free to mix and match across the chapters if you'd like to devise your own menu for a feast. For instance, you might want to put together a vegan or vegetarian feast, a gluten-free feast or a feast containing the recipes you like the best. Let your own palate be your guide.

You might notice that this book contains a large proportion of vegetarian recipes, although there are some very tasty chicken and fish dishes included, too. When I was growing up, chicken and fish were cooked only occasionally at home, as my father is vegetarian. And now, my husband is vegetarian, so my home cooking has always been heavily weighted towards vegetarian meals. This fact is, of course, reflected in all my books, including this one.

No matter how you choose to use the recipes in this book, I hope that these dishes will become part of the feasts you share in your own home, and contribute to the joy you experience with your family and friends as you gather together to celebrate good food and life.

The whole concept of the now-traditional British Friday night curry was totally new to me when I moved to the UK many years ago. Obviously, we had Indian food every day, so to dedicate one evening to Indian food was novel. The food on Indian takeaway menus was also new to me, as most of the dishes were not truly Indian. But I happily embraced this unique cuisine for its own merits, and in this chapter, I share my home-cooked versions of everyone's favourite Indian takeaway dishes. All these dishes complement one other, so if you're feeling adventurous, cook them all together for a big feast for your friends and family. Or cook them one at a time and enjoy your favourites again and again. I have tried to cater for all tastes here, and there are some great combinations of dishes to be had. The Dal Fry with the Ghobi 65 is sensational, or go for the Chicken Tikka Masala and Saag Alu. The Paneer Do Pyaza is divine with the Prawn Vindaloo. You'll love my version of Cumin Rice, which can be served with any of the curries, unless you prefer Peshawari Naan. Of course, I couldn't leave out my Onion Chickpea Bhajis. Finish the meal with the Double ka metha to complete the wholesome Indian takeaway vibe.

Friday night takeaway

Gobhi 65

Dal fry

Onion chickpea bhajis

Chicken tikka masala

Prawn vindaloo

Saag alu

Vegetable jalfrezi

Cumin rice

Paneer do pyaza

Peshawari naan

Double ka metha

This is my veggie take on the world-famous Indian-restaurant dish known as Chicken 65, the origin of which is hotly debated. Some say it was first served at a restaurant in Chennai where it was number 65 on the menu, while others say it is named after the 65 spices used to make it. Either way, it's delicious! Although my cauliflower version doesn't use 65 spices, I feel it captures something of the flavour of the popular chicken dish.

Gobhi 65

SERVES 4

sunflower oil, for deep-frying

1 cauliflower, cut into roughly 2.5-cm (1-in) florets

FOR THE BATTER

1-cm (½-in) piece of fresh root ginger, peeled and grated

2 tablespoons shop-bought chilli-garlic sauce

120g (4¼oz) cornflour

120g (4¼oz) rice flour

½ teaspoon salt

230ml (8fl oz) water

FOR THE STIR-FRY

2 tablespoons sunflower oil

2.5-cm (1-in) piece of fresh root ginger, peeled and julienned

8–10 fresh curry leaves

2 tablespoons shop-bought chilli-garlic sauce

2 tablespoons water

Put all the batter ingredients in a bowl and mix well with a spoon.

Heat the oil in a deep saucepan or deep-fat fryer to a cooking temperature of 170°C (340°F). (Maintain this throughout cooking.) Dip each cauliflower floret in the batter, then slide it carefully into the hot oil. Cook over a medium heat for a couple of minutes on each side until golden and crispy. Remove the cooked florets with a slotted spoon and transfer to a plate lined with kitchen paper to drain.

To make the stir-fry, heat the oil in a separate pan or a wok over a high heat. Add the ginger and curry leaves to the pan and let them sizzle for a minute, then add the chilli-garlic sauce, followed by the measured water. Allow the water to come to the boil, then add the fried cauliflower, stir quickly to cover the florets with the mixture in the pan, then remove from the pan and serve immediately.

FOR THE DAL

150g (5½oz) toor dal
(split pigeon peas)

50g (1¾oz) moong dal
(split mung beans)

50g (1¾oz) chana dal
(split yellow peas)

1 litre (1¾ pints) boiling
water

1 teaspoon salt

1 teaspoon ground turmeric

FOR THE FIRST TADKA

1 tablespoon ghee

1 tablespoon sunflower oil

1 teaspoon cumin seeds

2 garlic cloves, finely
chopped

1-cm (½-in) piece of fresh
root ginger, finely chopped

1 green chilli, finely chopped

1 onion, finely chopped

handful of coriander leaves,
finely chopped

FOR THE SECOND TADKA

2 tablespoons ghee

2 garlic cloves, thinly sliced

4 red chillies, thinly sliced

8–10 fresh curry leaves

You might have seen this dal dish on the menu of your local takeaway, and it's just as popular in India, where it is served at *dhabas* (small roadside eateries). What makes it so delicious is the double tadka – one is stirred through the cooked lentils and the other sits on top of the final dish, waiting for you to break into it and enjoy this delicious combination of three lentils.

Dal fry

To make the dal, put all three types of lentils into a saucepan and cover with the measured boiling water. Leave to soak for 1 hour. Stir in the salt and turmeric and cook over a medium–low heat for 40–45 minutes until the lentils are soft and mushy.

Make the first tadka towards the end of the cooking time for the dal. Heat the ghee and oil in a saucepan over a medium–low heat and add the cumin seeds. Once they begin to sizzle, add the garlic, ginger, chilli and onion and cook for 5–6 minutes until the onion begins to turn golden. Stir in the chopped coriander and mix well, then pour the tadka over the cooked dal in the saucepan and mix it in well. Transfer the dal to a serving bowl.

Now make the second tadka. Heat the ghee over a medium–low heat in the same pan you used to make the first tadka. Add the garlic and chillies and cook for a minute until they soften. Now mix in the curry leaves and let the tadka sizzle for a few seconds, then pour it over the dal and serve immediately.

I have yet to meet someone who doesn't enjoy a freshly cooked onion bhaji. It's such a great snack, starter, side dish – whichever way you like it. So, I've taken it up a notch in this recipe for all you bhaji connoisseurs! The addition of chickpeas makes these bhajis super-crispy as well as wholesome... and irresistible.

Onion chickpea bhajis

SERVES 4

2 onions, thinly sliced

120g (4¼oz) gram flour

1 teaspoon salt

1 teaspoon garam masala

1 teaspoon chaat masala

1-cm (½-in) piece of fresh root ginger, peeled and grated

400g (14oz) can of chickpeas, drained and rinsed

4 tablespoons water

sunflower oil, for deep-frying

Put the onions, gram flour, salt, dry spices and ginger into a bowl. Using your hands, squash the onions into the flour so that it becomes a little sticky.

Put the chickpeas into a separate bowl and, using a potato masher, mash them slightly – don't completely squash them. Add these to the bowl with the onion mixture, then slowly add the measured water, mixing with your hands as you go. You want just enough water to make the batter sticky but not watery.

Heat the oil in a deep saucepan or deep-fat fryer to a cooking temperature of 170°C (340°F). (Maintain this temperature throughout cooking.) Once the oil reaches cooking temperature, carefully add a small batch of the bhajis to the oil, sliding them in one piece at a time – it's up to you what size to make your bhajis, but I recommend lime-size portions (a tablespoonful of the mixture). Flatten the bhajis slightly with your fingers before you put them into the hot oil. Cook for 2 minutes on each side until nicely golden and crispy. Using a slotted spoon, transfer the bhajis to a plate lined with kitchen paper. Leave to drain while you cook subsequent batches, then serve immediately with your choice of dipping sauce.

If a restaurant has chicken tikka masala on the menu, chances are I will be ordering it. This version is an absolute winner. Cashew nuts make the spicy sauce wonderfully creamy and an ideal partner for the tasty oven-cooked chicken. Or you could leave out the masala and serve the chicken on its own – cook it on the barbecue to add that wonderful smokiness and make it more like a classic chicken tikka. To turn it into a chaat, sprinkle chaat masala and a squeeze of lemon juice over the chicken pieces and serve as a snack or starter. But make sure you try this curry, too. It's too good to miss out on.

Chicken tikka masala

SERVES 4

FOR THE CHICKEN

200ml (7fl oz) natural yogurt

4 garlic cloves, grated

1-cm (½-in) piece of fresh root ginger, peeled and grated

1 teaspoon garam masala

1 teaspoon chilli powder

½ teaspoon salt

8 boneless, skinless chicken thighs, cut into roughly 4-cm (1½-in) pieces

FOR THE CREAMY MASALA PURÉE

3 tablespoons sunflower oil

1 cinnamon stick

4 cardamom pods

1 bay leaf

4 cloves

12 cashew nuts

2 onions, roughly chopped

2.5-cm (1-in) piece of fresh root ginger, peeled and roughly chopped

First, prepare the marinade for the chicken. Mix the yogurt, garlic, ginger, garam masala, chilli powder and salt in a bowl. Add the chicken pieces and ensure they are coated in the marinade, then cover the bowl and leave to rest in the refrigerator for a minimum of 1 hour or overnight.

While the chicken is marinating, make the creamy masala purée. Heat the oil in a saucepan and add the whole spices and cashew nuts. Let them sizzle for a few seconds, then add the onions and cook over a medium–low heat for 8–10 minutes until golden. Now add the ginger, garlic and chilli and cook for another minute, then stir in the tomatoes. Cover the pan with a lid and cook over a low heat for 20 minutes until the tomato, onions and nuts are all softened and cooked through. Take the pan off the heat and set aside to cool slightly, then blitz to a purée in a blender or small food processor.

4 garlic cloves, roughly chopped

1 red chilli, roughly chopped

4 tomatoes, roughly chopped

FOR THE MASALA

2 tablespoons sunflower oil

2 onions, cut into chunks

1 quantity Creamy Masala Purée (see opposite)

¾ teaspoon salt

½ teaspoon caster sugar

1 teaspoon ground turmeric

1 teaspoon garam masala

2 teaspoons ground coriander

1 teaspoon chilli powder

1 tablespoon dried fenugreek leaves (kasuri methi)

When you are ready to cook the chicken, preheat the oven to 200°C (400°F), Gas Mark 6. Place the chicken with all the marinade on a baking tray and roast for 25 minutes.

While the chicken is cooking, make the masala. Heat the oil in a saucepan over a medium–low heat and add the onion chunks. Cook for 5 minutes until softened. Now add the creamy masala purée, then the salt, sugar and all the spices and mix well. Cover the pan with a lid and cook over a low heat for 10 minutes to allow the flavours to infuse the sauce.

Now add the chicken with all the juices from the baking tray to the pan. Increase the heat to medium and cook for 5 minutes. Serve immediately.

See photograph overleaf.

Vindaloo comes from Goa. Some say it can be traced back to a dish brought to Goa by the Portuguese, to which the Indians added tons of spices – and the famous vindaloo was born! This amazing curry is made with a paste of deeply aromatic spices. My version is simpler than the classic dish, and made with prawns instead of the traditional meat because I love how they soak up all the flavours in the curry.

Prawn vindaloo

SERVES 4

1 tablespoon sunflower oil

2 tablespoons ghee

1 teaspoon mustard seeds

1 onion, finely chopped

1 tomato, finely chopped

100ml (3½fl oz) water

½ teaspoon salt

1 teaspoon chilli powder

16 raw king prawns, peeled and deveined, tails left intact

FOR THE CURRY PASTE

1 teaspoon coriander seeds

1 teaspoon cumin seeds

2 cardamom pods

2 cloves

1-cm (½-in) piece of fresh root ginger

4 garlic cloves

6 dried chillies

1 teaspoon soft brown sugar

½ teaspoon ground turmeric

1 teaspoon cider vinegar

4 tablespoons water

First, make the curry paste. Put the coriander and cumin seeds, cardamom pods and cloves into a frying pan set over a low heat and toast for about 2 minutes until they become aromatic and begin to change colour.

Transfer the toasted spices to the bowl of a blender. Add the ginger, garlic, dried chillies, sugar and ground turmeric and blitz the mixture to a paste. Next, add the vinegar and measured water and blitz again to mix well. Set aside.

To make the curry, heat the oil and ghee in a saucepan over a medium–low heat. Add the mustard seeds and cook for a few seconds until they begin to pop. Now stir in the onion and cook for 5 minutes until it softens. Next, mix in the curry paste, then the tomato. Stir in the measured water, cover the pan with a lid and cook over a low heat for 10 minutes until the tomato is soft and mushy.

Add the salt and chilli powder to the pan and mix well. Now carefully stir in the prawns, ensuring they are coated in the masala, and cook for 3–4 minutes until the prawns have turned pink and are done. Serve immediately.

Growing up in India, *saag* to me meant mustard leaves, and saag alu (potato and mustard greens curry) was made often in the winter months when the greens were in season. When I moved to the UK, I discovered that a dish called saag alu was popular in Indian restaurants, but was surprised to learn it was made with spinach leaves, not mustard greens. I would call this palak alu (*palak* means spinach in Hindi). But whatever you call it, this is a delicious dish that is great served with some naan or rice. The simple spicing makes it very easy to prepare, too.

Saag alu

SERVES 4

2 tablespoons sunflower oil

1 teaspoon mustard seeds

1 teaspoon cumin seeds

1 onion, finely chopped

1-cm (½-in) piece of fresh root ginger, julienned

2 garlic cloves, thinly sliced

2 tomatoes, finely chopped

1 teaspoon chilli powder

½ teaspoon ground turmeric

1 teaspoon garam masala

½ teaspoon salt

2 medium potatoes, peeled and cut into 2.5-cm (1-in) pieces

100ml (3½fl oz) water

400g (14oz) spinach leaves, finely chopped

2 tablespoons lemon juice

Heat the oil in a saucepan over a low heat. Add the mustard and cumin seeds and cook for a few seconds until they begin to sizzle. Now add the onion and cook for 5 minutes until softened and beginning to colour.

Stir the ginger and garlic into the pan and cook for 1 minute more. Next, mix in the tomatoes, the spices and salt, increase the heat to high and cook for 1 minute. Now stir in the potatoes and measured water, cover the pan with a lid and cook over a low heat for 10 minutes until the potatoes are soft and cooked through.

Now add the spinach to the pan, mix well, cover the pan with a lid and cook over a low heat for 5 minutes until the spinach has wilted. Take the pan off the heat, stir in the lemon juice and serve immediately.

I don't know the exact origin of this dish, but I do know that *jal* means hot in Bengali, and I'm guessing that *frezi* is an Indian way of saying stir-fry. One story states that, like butter chicken, jalfrezi was invented to use up leftover meats. Good reasons bearing good results! This popular Indian takeaway dish is full of flavour. I love my vegetarian version – the curry is a great base for these vegetables – but you can use chicken or paneer instead of the vegetables if you like. And feel free to reduce the heat by skipping the green chillies.

Vegetable jalfrezi

SERVES 4

4 tablespoons sunflower oil

2 onions, thinly sliced

2 onions, finely chopped

2 green chillies, finely chopped

4 garlic cloves, finely chopped

2.5-cm (1-in) piece of fresh root ginger, finely chopped

4 tomatoes, finely chopped

200ml (7fl oz) water

1 teaspoon salt

1 teaspoon chilli powder

½ teaspoon ground turmeric

1 teaspoon ground coriander

1 teaspoon garam masala

2 tablespoons tomato ketchup

175g (6oz) baby corn, halved lengthways

200g (7oz) mangetout, trimmed

220g (7¾oz) green beans, halved

Heat the oil in a saucepan, then add the thinly sliced onions and cook over a medium heat for 5 minutes until they begin to change colour. Using a slotted spoon, scoop them out of the oil, place them in a bowl and set aside.

Return the pan to the heat and stir the chopped onions into the remaining oil. Cook over a medium– low heat for 8–10 minutes until deeply golden. Now add the chillies, garlic and ginger and cook for 1 minute. Next, mix in the tomatoes and half the measured water, cover the pan with a lid and cook over a low heat for 20 minutes until the tomatoes are cooked down and mushy and the oil has separated from them.

Stir the salt and spices into the mixture in the pan and cook for 1 minute, then mix in the ketchup and remaining water and bring to the boil. Now stir in the veg, cover the pan with a lid and cook over a low heat for 20 minutes until the veg is cooked through. Stir in the reserved fried onions and serve immediately.

As the name suggests, this dish has tons of cumin in it – both whole and ground seeds – giving it a wonderful earthy, comforting warmth. Try it as a simple rice accompaniment for all the lovely curries in this book. To be honest, I'd happily eat this rice with just some yogurt.

Cumin rice

SERVES 4

1 tablespoon sunflower oil

1 tablespoon ghee

2 teaspoons cumin seeds

1½ teaspoons salt

300g (10½oz) basmati rice, washed and drained

1 teaspoon ground cumin

1 teaspoon chilli powder

20g (¾oz) coriander leaves, finely chopped, plus extra to garnish

700ml (1¼ pints) boiling water

Heat the oil and ghee in a saucepan over a medium–low heat, then add the cumin seeds. Cook for a few seconds until they begin to sizzle. Stir in the salt, then add the rice and stir well. Next, add the spices and coriander, then the measured boiling water. Cover the pan with a lid and cook over a low heat for 15 minutes.

Once the cooking time has elapsed, turn off the heat but don't lift off the lid. Leave the rice to rest for 15 minutes, then garnish with extra chopped coriander leaves before serving.

4 tablespoons sunflower oil

10 baby shallots

¼ teaspoon salt

¼ teaspoon ground turmeric

¼ teaspoon chilli powder

450g (1lb) paneer, cut into 2.5-cm (1-in) cubes

FOR THE CURRY

4 tablespoons sunflower oil

2 tablespoons salted butter

1 teaspoon cumin seeds

1 cinnamon stick

4 cardamom pods

2 onions, finely chopped

4 garlic cloves, finely chopped

2.5-cm (1-in) piece of fresh root ginger, peeled and finely chopped

1 green chilli, thinly sliced

2 tomatoes, finely chopped

200ml (7fl oz) water

1 teaspoon chilli powder

½ teaspoon ground turmeric

2 teaspoons ground coriander

1 teaspoon ground cumin

100ml (3½fl oz) natural yogurt

2 tablespoons dried fenugreek leaves (kasuri methi)

This is one of my favourite paneer dishes. *Do pyaza* means two onions – I'm not sure why the dish has this name because, usually, there are definitely more than two onions used. Perhaps it is because onions are added at two stages, but who knows? I love onions in anything, even when used raw (the Red Onion Salad on page 124 is one of my favourites), and the baby shallots in this curry are simply delicious. If you fancy a change, you can cook the curry with chicken or some potatoes.

Paneer do pyaza

Heat 3 tablespoons of the oil in a saucepan and add the shallots. Cook over a medium–low heat for 6–8 minutes until the shallots are nicely softened. Transfer to a bowl and set aside.

Put the salt, turmeric, chilli powder and remaining oil into a bowl and mix well. Now add the paneer cubes to the bowl and coat them well in the spices. Put the paneer cubes into the hot pan you used to cook the shallots and cook over a medium–low heat for 1–2 minutes on each side until lightly golden. Add the paneer to the bowl with the shallots.

Return the pan to the heat as you'll now be cooking the curry in it. Set it over a medium–low heat, add the oil and butter and, once hot, add the cumin seeds and the whole spices to the pan. Allow them to sizzle for a few seconds, then add the onions. Cook over a medium–low heat for 8–10 minutes until the onions are golden. Next, add the garlic, ginger and chilli and cook for another minute.

Now stir in the tomatoes along with half the measured water. Cover the pan with a lid and cook over a low heat for 15 minutes until the onions are completely cooked down and the oil is pooling at the sides of the pan.

Stir all the spices into the pan, then take it off the heat. Add the yogurt and remaining water and stir for a few seconds, then return the pan to the heat. Add the fenugreek leaves and the shallots and paneer, then mix well. Cover the pan with the lid and cook over a low heat for 5 minutes until the shallots and paneer are heated through. Serve immediately.

A classic takeaway favourite, this naan is made with yeasted dough and filled with an unusual combination of coconut and raisins or sultanas. It isn't dessert-like, but has a pleasing sweetness that acts as the perfect foil for a rich savoury dish. It is said to have originated in Peshawar, a city in Pakistan, and some say it's a version of a naan originally made in Kashmir. All I know is that it's a great accompaniment to a spicy curry or enjoyable with just a lovely chutney or pickle.

Peshawari naan

MAKES 6

250g (9oz) strong white bread flour, plus extra for dusting

½ teaspoon salt

½ teaspoon granulated sugar

7g (¼oz) fast-action dried yeast

120ml (4fl oz) water

salted butter, melted, to serve

FOR THE FILLING

50g (1¾oz) sultanas

50g (1¾oz) desiccated coconut

50g (1¾oz) ground almonds

Put the flour, salt, sugar and yeast into a bowl and mix well. Now add the measured water a little at a time, and bring the mixture together to form a soft dough. Knead for 5 minutes until the dough is slightly smoother, then cover the bowl with a clean tea towel and leave to prove for 1 hour.

Put the filling ingredients into the bowl of a blender and blitz together until coarsely ground.

Divide the dough into 6 equal portions. Roll out each portion on a lightly floured surface into a small circle with a diameter of roughly 7.5–10cm (3–4in).

Working with 1 dough portion at a time, place 2 tablespoons of the filling in the centre of each dough circle, then gather the sides of the circle up around the filling and press the dough at the top of the ball to seal the filling within the dough. Now carefully roll the ball into a small circle or oval shape with a diameter of 13–15cm (5–6in), being careful not to tear the dough and reveal the filling.

Heat the grill on a medium setting. Place the naans on a baking sheet and grill for 1 minute or until golden. Turn them over and grill for another minute. Once cooked, brush each naan with some melted butter and serve immediately.

This popular takeaway treat (and the very similar shahi tukda) is a deep-fried bread that is soaked in sugar syrup, then topped with *rabdi* (Indian thickened milk). My simplified version uses an easy thickened milk instead of *rabdi* and skips the sugar-syrup steeping to keep it less sweet. You can prepare the thickened milk beforehand, then fry the bread fresh when you are ready to serve it.

Double ka metha

SERVES 4

8 slices of white bread, crusts removed

ghee, for deep-frying

8–10 almonds, thinly sliced

8–10 pistachio nuts, thinly sliced

FOR THE THICKENED CARDAMOM MILK

400ml (14fl oz) milk

2 tablespoons ground almonds

2 tablespoons milk powder

2 tablespoons condensed milk

½ teaspoon ground cardamom

To prepare the thickened cardamom milk, put the milk into a saucepan and bring it to the boil over a medium heat. Cook over a low heat for 10 minutes. Stir in the ground almonds and cook over a low heat for 5 minutes. Mix in the milk powder and condensed milk and continue to cook over a low heat for 10 minutes, stirring every couple of minutes. Now take the pan off the heat, stir in the ground cardamom and set aside.

Cut each slice of bread into 4 triangles. Heat the ghee in a deep saucepan or deep-fat fryer to a cooking temperature of 170–180°C (340–350°F). (Maintain this temperature range throughout cooking.) Add the bread slices and cook for 1 minute or so on each side until golden and crispy.

Transfer the fried bread triangles to a serving plate and pour the thickened cardamom milk over the top. Sprinkle over the sliced nuts and serve immediately.

This is my absolute favourite Indian food. There's something so exciting about chaat – it is spicy, sweet, sour and everything in between. The crunchy onions, fresh coriander, crispy sev...it's like an orchestra of flavours in your mouth. I could happily live on chaat forever (which is why I wrote another book all about it, called *Chai, Chaat & Chutney*). I found it a major challenge to restrict chaat recipes to this one chapter alone, but I've tried to share with you a bit of everything. I adore the deep-fried Khasta Kachori, both as it is or assembled as a chaat. The light and crispy Spinach Leaf Pakora are so delicious, I highly recommend you double up the quantities, because these pakoras tend to disappear within seconds of cooking. I've included super-crispy and irresistible Smashed Alu Tikki, and wholesome Dahi Vada Chaat, which is quite a feast in itself. The Dal Papdi Chaat is, for sure, my personal weakness, and the Dahi Puri is always a crowd-pleaser. Go for the Fruit Chaat if you're looking for something light and fresh. Feel free to mix and match any of these dishes, or serve them individually to really savour your favourites. Enjoy a lovely Cumin Ginger Lassi alongside your feast, and finish off with the creamy Pista Kulfi for a true taste of Indian street food.

Chaat

Dal papdi chaat

Smashed alu tikki

Dahi puri

Khasta kachori

Spinach leaf pakora

Dahi vada chaat

Tamarind jaggery chutney

Coriander yogurt chutney

Fruit chaat

Pista kulfi

Cumin ginger lassi

FOR THE PAPDI

300g (10½oz) plain flour, plus extra for dusting

½ teaspoon salt

½ teaspoon chilli powder

½ teaspoon ground cumin

3 tablespoons sunflower oil, plus extra for deep-frying

120ml (4fl oz) water

FOR THE DAL

250g (9oz) chana dal (split yellow peas)

1 litre (1¾ pints) boiling water

1 teaspoon salt

½ teaspoon ground turmeric

2 tablespoons ghee

1 green chilli, finely chopped

1 teaspoon ground cumin

1 teaspoon chaat masala

TO SERVE

100ml (3½fl oz) natural yogurt

50ml (2fl oz) water

Tamarind Jaggery Chutney (see page 53), to taste

Coriander Yogurt Chutney (see page 54), to taste

pinch of salt

pinch of chilli powder

1 red onion, finely chopped

1 green chilli, finely chopped

This is one of those dishes that I could happily live off for the rest of my life. The crispness of the papdi with the moreish masala dal and the magical chutneys is the most dreamy combination of all! You can prepare the papdi, dal and chutneys in advance, but put the dish together only when you are ready to eat to retain the satisfying crispiness of the papdi.

Dal papdi chaat

Start by preparing the papdi. Put the flour, salt, chilli powder, cumin and oil into a bowl and mix well. Slowly add the measured water as you mix with your hand to form a soft dough. Knead the dough for 2 minutes. Cover the bowl with a clean tea towel and leave to rest for 15 minutes.

Heat the oil in a deep saucepan or deep-fat fryer to a cooking temperature of 170°C (340°F). (Maintain this temperature throughout cooking.)

Meanwhile, divide the dough into 4 equal portions and roll out each portion on a lightly floured surface into a thin sheet (in any shape you like) to a depth of roughly 2mm (1/16in). Now cut these sheets into thin strips, diamond shapes or squares. Place the shapes carefully into the hot oil and fry over a medium–low heat for 3–4 minutes until golden and crispy. Remove the papdi from the hot oil using a slotted spoon, transfer

to a plate lined with kitchen paper and leave to cool while you prepare the dal.

Put the chana dal into a pan with the measured boiling water, salt and turmeric and cook over a medium–low heat for 1 hour until the dal is soft. If it becomes too thick during cooking, stir in another 100ml (3½fl oz) boiling water.

Heat the ghee in a small saucepan, then add the chilli. Once the ghee begins to sizzle, take the pan off the heat, add the cumin and chaat masala and mix well. Pour this mixture over the cooked dal and mix well. Leave to cool slightly.

When you're ready to serve, put the yogurt into a bowl and stir in the measured water to thin it out.

Place the cooled papdis on a plate, top with the warm dal, then drizzle over the yogurt and chutneys. Sprinkle with the salt and chilli powder, then the onion and green chilli. Serve immediately.

Alu tikki is one of the most popular chaats in India and beyond, and it's certainly high up there on my list, too. Often on street corners you can find vendors selling this tikki chaat. They semi-prepare the potato cutlets, half-cooking them in small balls. As soon as you place an order, they turn up the heat, squash the tikkis and fry them until crispy and golden. I usually prepare this dish as a chaat, but you can serve the tikkis without the toppings as a snack or a party canapé.

Smashed alu tikki

MAKES 8

4 medium potatoes, peeled and cut into quarters

¾ teaspoon salt

¾ teaspoon chilli powder

4 tablespoons cornflour

8 tablespoons sunflower oil

TO SERVE

150ml (¼ pint) natural yogurt

50ml (2fl oz) water

pinch of salt

pinch of chilli powder

pinch of chaat masala

Coriander Yogurt Chutney (see page 54), to taste

Tamarind Jaggery Chutney (see page 53), to taste

Cook the potatoes in a saucepan of boiling water until cooked through and soft. Drain, set aside in a bowl until cool enough to handle, then mash them with a potato masher. Now add the salt, chilli powder and cornflour to the mash and mix it all well. Divide the mixture into 8 portions and shape them into balls.

Heat 2 tablespoons of the oil in a frying pan over a low heat. Add 4 potato balls and cook for 2 minutes on each side until lightly golden. Now add 2 more tablespoons oil to the pan and, using the back of a large metal or wooden spoon, flatten the balls into flat cakes. Increase the heat to medium and cook for 2 minutes on each side until deep golden brown. Repeat with the remaining 4 potato balls to complete frying the tikkis.

Put the yogurt into a bowl, add the measured water and whisk until the mixture is smooth.

Place the tikkis on a serving plate and drizzle over the yogurt. Sprinkle the salt, chilli powder and chaat masala on top. Now drizzle over the chutneys and serve immediately.

This dahi puri is a version of the popular snack pani puri, but instead of spicy water, the puri is filled with yogurt before being topped with a medley of flavours. Puris are readily available in Asian shops by the name of pani puri, as is 'nylon' sev, which is just a quirky name for superfine sev, a crunchy snack made with gram (chickpea) flour. You can prepare all the elements beforehand, but put the dish together just before serving so that it retains its satisfying crispiness.

Dahi puri

SERVES 4

1 medium potato, peeled, boiled and cooled

50ml (2fl oz) water

200ml (7fl oz) natural yogurt

24 puris (pani puri)

Tamarind Jaggery Chutney (see page 53), to taste

Coriander Yogurt Chutney (see page 54), to taste

¼ teaspoon salt

¼ teaspoon chilli powder

¼ teaspoon chaat masala

nylon sev (gram flour noodles), to taste

Break up the boiled potato roughly by hand.

Whisk the measured water and yogurt in a bowl until the mixture is smooth.

When you are ready to serve, place the puris on a dish and, using your thumb, gently break the top of each one to make a small opening. Load up each puri with a little of the potato, then add a good tablespoon or more of the yogurt on top. Now drizzle over some of the tamarind and coriander chutneys. Sprinkle the salt, chilli powder and chaat masala on top, then scatter the sev over the puris to finish. Serve immediately.

Khasta means crispy in Hindi, so these crisp, golden and delicious pastries are aptly named. All over India, you'll find kachoris with different fillings – variations on lentils, nuts or flour pastes. This version is filled with a delicious mixture of mung beans and gram flour. Kachoris are amazing hot, but they are also great when served at room temperature, so you can prepare them in advance for your feast. You can also make what we call a full chaat with these kachoris by breaking them up and topping with some Coriander Yogurt Chutney (see page 54) and Tamarind Jaggery Chutney (see page 53).

Khasta kachori

MAKES 15

FOR THE DOUGH

300g (10½oz) plain flour, plus extra for dusting

½ teaspoon salt

4 tablespoons ghee

approximately 4 tablespoons water

FOR THE FILLING

160g (5¾oz) moong dal (split mung beans)

2 tablespoons coriander seeds

1 tablespoon fennel seeds

1 teaspoon cumin seeds

3 tablespoons sunflower oil, plus extra for deep-frying

pinch of asafoetida

½ teaspoon salt

½ teaspoon garam masala

60g (2¼oz) gram flour

2.5-cm (1-in) piece of fresh root ginger, peeled and grated

1 green chilli, finely chopped

To make the filling, put the moong dal into a heatproof bowl, cover with boiling water and leave to soak for 1 hour. After the soaking time for the lentils has elapsed, drain them, transfer to the bowl of a blender and blitz to a very coarse mixture – don't allow it to become a paste.

While the lentils are soaking, prepare the dough. Put the flour and salt into a mixing bowl, then rub in the ghee with your fingers until the mixture has the texture of breadcrumbs. Next, mix in just enough of the measured water (or more, if necessary), a little at a time, until you have a soft dough. Leave the dough in the mixing bowl, cover the bowl with a clean tea towel and leave to rest for at least 30 minutes.

While the dough rests, continue making the filling. Heat a saucepan over a low heat, then add the coriander, fennel and cumin seeds and dry-roast for 2 minutes until they become aromatic and begin to change colour. Remove the toasted seeds from the pan and blitz them to a powder in a spice grinder. Alternatively, pound them to a powder using a pestle and mortar.

In the same pan, heat the oil over a very low heat. Stir in the asafoetida and, after a few seconds, add the ground

seeds. Immediately add the salt and garam masala, followed by the gram flour. Continue to cook over a low heat for 5 minutes until the gram flour starts to change colour.

Add the blitzed lentils, ginger and chilli to the pan and cook over a low heat for 5 minutes until the lentils look dried out. Take the pan off the heat and set aside to allow the mixture to cool.

Divide the dough and the filling into roughly 15 portions. Roll out each portion of dough on a lightly floured surface into a small circle around 5–6cm (2–2½in) in diameter. Place a portion of the filling in the centre of each dough circle, then gather the edges of the dough around the filling and press the ball on top to seal. Roll each ball gently into a small circle with a diameter of 5–6cm (2–2½in).

Heat the oil in a deep saucepan or deep-fat fryer to a cooking temperature of approximately 160°C (325°F). (Maintain this temperature throughout cooking.) Carefully slide a few kachoris at a time into the pan and cook for 3–4 minutes on each side until crispy and golden. Using a slotted spoon, transfer the kachoris to a plate lined with kitchen paper to drain.

See photograph overleaf.

This form of pakora is very popular both as a street food and in restaurants in India. You can eat spinach pakoras as they come, piping hot out of the pan, or top them with some Coriander Yogurt Chutney (see page 54) and Tamarind Jaggery Chutney (see page 53) for a tasty chaat. These crispy snacks are very moreish, so be warned – it's difficult to stop at one or two!

Spinach leaf pakora

SERVES 4

120g (4¼oz) gram flour

½ teaspoon salt, plus extra to serve

¼ teaspoon ground turmeric

¼ teaspoon chilli powder

1-cm (½-in) piece of fresh root ginger, peeled and grated

1 green chilli, finely chopped

120ml (4fl oz) water

sunflower oil, for deep-frying

50g (1¾oz) baby spinach leaves

Mix the gram flour, salt, spices, ginger and green chilli in a mixing bowl, then slowly add the measured water and mix well so that there are no lumps in the batter.

Heat the oil in a deep saucepan or deep-fat fryer to a cooking temperature of 170–180°C (340–350°F). (Maintain this temperature range throughout cooking.) One by one, dip the spinach leaves in the batter, then carefully lower them into the hot oil. Cook for a minute or less, and then turn them over and cook for another minute until golden and crispy. Using a slotted spoon, transfer the pakoras to a bowl lined with kitchen paper to drain, then sprinkle with salt and serve immediately.

Dahi vada is a popular chaat as well as an important element of the feast table at many weddings and festivals, when it is served alongside an array of delicious dishes. Usually, urad dal is used to make the vadas, but for this recipe, I use a combination of two different lentils for a slightly different texture and flavour. You can prepare the vadas two to three days in advance and let them chill in the refrigerator until ready to serve, then quickly assemble the dish at the last minute.

Dahi vada chaat

SERVES 4–6

150g (5½oz) moong dal (split mung beans)

100g (3½oz) chana dal (split yellow peas)

1-cm (½-in) piece of fresh root ginger, peeled and roughly chopped

sunflower oil, for deep-frying

1 teaspoon salt

200ml (7fl oz) natural yogurt

100ml (3½fl oz) water

½ teaspoon ground cumin

Tamarind Jaggery Chutney (see page 53), to taste

handful of coriander leaves, finely chopped

8–10 mint leaves, finely chopped

handful of fresh pomegranate seeds

10–12 Papdi (see page 40) (optional)

Soak the moong dal and chana dal in warm water for 3–4 hours or overnight.

Drain the lentils, place them in the bowl of a blender, add the ginger and blitz to a smooth paste. Now transfer the mixture to a bowl and whisk for 5 minutes to incorporate some air into it – this will help to give the vadas a soft texture.

Heat the oil in a deep saucepan or deep-fat fryer to a cooking temperature of 160°C (325°F). (Maintain this temperature throughout cooking.)

Scoop up lemon-size portions of the vada batter and carefully slide them into the hot oil one by one. Cook for 2–3 minutes until very lightly golden.

Meanwhile, select a heatproof bowl that is large enough to hold all the vadas and put some warm water into it. Stir in ½ teaspoon of the salt. Using a slotted spoon, remove the vadas from the hot oil and put them directly into

the water bowl, ensuring they are all submerged. Leave to stand for 5 minutes. This will help to keep the vadas soft and spongy so that they will absorb the yogurt.

After the standing time has elapsed, the vadas will be cool enough to handle. Carefully squeeze out the excess water from each vada and place it on a shallow serving tray.

Mix the yogurt, measured water, remaining salt and the cumin in a bowl. Pour this mixture over the squeezed vadas. Now drizzle the tamarind chutney on top, then scatter over the chopped coriander and mint and the pomegranate seeds. You can also sprinkle the broken-up papdi on top for a lovely crunchy finish, if liked.

The most vital ingredient in any chaat, this chutney is sour, sweet and spicy all at once, making it utterly delicious and irresistible. Don't save it just for chaat – it goes ridiculously well with just about any savoury meal or snack!

Tamarind jaggery chutney

500ml (18fl oz) boiling water

10 medjool dates, pitted and roughly chopped

100g (3½oz) jaggery, roughly chopped

4 tablespoons tamarind paste

1 tablespoon fennel seeds

1 tablespoon cumin seeds

½ teaspoon salt

1 teaspoon chilli powder

Put the measured boiling water into a saucepan with the dates and jaggery. Cook over a low heat for 10–15 minutes until the dates have softened completely. Now add the tamarind paste and cook over a low heat for a further 15–20 minutes.

Meanwhile, toast the fennel and cumin seeds in a frying pan over a low heat for a couple of minutes until they become aromatic and begin to change colour. Then, using a pestle and mortar, crush them to a coarse powder.

Pass the tamarind mixture through a sieve, then return it to the pan. Add the salt, chilli powder and the powdered toasted seeds and cook for a minute over a low heat. Take the pan off the heat and leave the chutney to cool to room temperature before serving. You can store this chutney in an airtight container in the refrigerator for up to 1 month.

I know many other Indians who simply can't sit down to a meal without a coriander chutney on the table, and this particular version is a staple in my home. It's easy to make, creamier than my other chutneys, yet fresh and light.

Coriander yogurt chutney

50g (1¾oz) coriander leaves

20g (¾oz) mint leaves

4 green chillies, roughly chopped

1-cm (½-in) piece of fresh root ginger, peeled and roughly chopped

juice of 1 lime

1 tablespoon water

1 teaspoon salt

1 teaspoon granulated sugar

2 tablespoons natural yogurt

Put all the ingredients, except the yogurt, into the bowl of a blender and blitz to a purée. Now add the yogurt and blitz again to incorporate it.

This chutney is best when served immediately after making, but you can store leftovers in an airtight container in the refrigerator for 3–4 days – it will still be tasty.

Spice up a simple bowl of fruit to make it even more refreshing. The sour, zingy spices work beautifully with the sweet, crisp freshness of the fruit. Fruit chaat is a popular Indian street food, and vendors often vary the spice blend to suit the combination of fruits. I'm a big fan of this particular combo.

Fruit chaat

SERVES 4

1 banana, peeled and roughly chopped

1 apple, cored and roughly chopped

seeds from ½ pomegranate

½ yellow-fleshed cantaloupe melon, peeled, deseeded and roughly chopped

couple of watermelon slices, peeled, deseeded and roughly chopped

1 orange, peeled, deseeded and roughly chopped

½ teaspoon kala namak (black salt)

½ teaspoon chaat masala

¼ teaspoon chilli flakes

pinch of salt

pinch of freshly ground black pepper

2 tablespoons lemon juice

Put all the prepared fruits into a bowl, add the spices, salt and pepper and lemon juice, then mix well. Serve immediately.

The real kulfi is made by cooking down milk gently for over an hour. In India, some people add milk solids, known as *khoya* or *mawa*, to the thickened milk, but milk solids are not always easily available in other countries, which is why I like to use this quicker version of kulfi. It is super-easy to make and tastes just as delicious as the real thing. Once you have made the base, feel free to add your own flavours instead of the pistachio – why not try rose (using rosewater), almonds or cashew nuts?

Pista kulfi

MAKES 8 SERVINGS

200ml (7fl oz) milk

200ml (7fl oz) double cream

½ teaspoon ground cardamom

2 tablespoons milk powder

100ml (3½fl oz) condensed milk

30g (1oz) pistachio nuts, crushed to a coarse powder, plus extra lightly crushed pieces to decorate

Put the milk and cream into a saucepan. Bring to the boil over a low heat, then cook over a low heat for 5 minutes.

Add the cardamom, milk powder and condensed milk to the pan and mix well, then continue to cook over a low heat for 15 minutes.

Take the pan off the heat and stir in the pistachio powder. Mix well, then set aside to cool completely.

You can use proper cone-shaped kulfi moulds, ice-lolly moulds or a plastic or glass freezer-proof container in which to freeze the kulfi. If using moulds, divide the mixture between 8 moulds, seal and freeze overnight. When ready to serve, dip the moulds in boiling water for 2 seconds, then slide the kulfi out of the mould (onto a serving plate, if using kulfi moulds) and serve immediately, decorated with crushed pistachio nuts.

Lassi is very popular in India during the summer months – drinking a long, cool glass of it is a great way to beat the extreme heat. You can find many varieties of lassi at street stalls and in restaurants, both sweet and savoury. Indeed, there's a famous lassi vendor in every town and city! I love this savoury version, which you can serve alongside a meal or on its own as a refreshment at any time.

Cumin ginger lassi

SERVES 4

1 teaspoon cumin seeds

250ml (9fl oz) natural yogurt

1-cm (½-in) piece of fresh root ginger, peeled and grated

1 green chilli, finely chopped

½ teaspoon salt

400ml (14fl oz) chilled water

Toast the cumin seeds in a pan over a low heat for a couple of minutes until they begin to change colour. Using a pestle and mortar, crush the toasted seeds to a coarse powder.

In a jug, whisk the yogurt with the ginger, chilli, salt and most of the cumin (save some to decorate). Now add the measured water and whisk until combined well. Pour the drink into 4 glasses, sprinkle with the remaining ground cumin and serve immediately.

I often write recipes that yield enough servings for four people. It's largely out of habit, as there are four of us at home. But some of my readers might find recipes for two more useful, so if you're cooking a slap-up feast for just you and a friend or loved one, you've come to the right chapter. Each recipe will yield enough to comfortably feed two if you are only making that one dish. If you decide to cook the whole menu, I suggest you halve the quantities and loosen your waistbands. But chances are you're cooking just one or two dishes from this menu at a time, and that will provide a lovely feast for you both. There is a bit of everything here for you to choose from. If you need snacks for a special afternoon spent with a friend, try the wonderful Potato-stuffed Onion Rings or the Fish Fry, either of which can be paired with the Chana Dal Chutney. My favourite dish is the Sticky Spicy Chicken Wings with Tomato Curry. Serve it with the Aubergine Coconut Rice. Spicy, Sour and Sweet Dal goes well with the rice dish, too, and also with the Roasted Cauliflower Salad and Spinach Onion Paratha. The Roasted Garlic Raita is stunning. Serve it alongside the Okra Masala with the paratha for a great combination. Lastly, if you make the cheesecake, I promise you will be making it again and again.

Feasts for two

Spicy, sour and sweet dal

Roasted cauliflower salad

Potato-stuffed onion rings

Sticky spicy chicken wings
with tomato curry

Okra masala

Fish fry

Aubergine coconut rice

Spinach onion paratha

Roasted garlic raita

Chana dal chutney

Biscoff cheesecake delight

I love lentils of any kind, and there are so many different colours and flavours to choose from. Of all of them, red lentils are probably the most readily available in the West, and they take the least amount of time to cook. I have chosen them for this recipe for their somewhat nutty flavour, which goes well with sour tamarind and sweet jaggery, giving this dish a rounded taste and a good dose of umami.

Spicy, sour and sweet dal

SERVES 2

FOR THE DAL

150g (5½oz) masoor dal (red lentils)

¾ teaspoon salt

¾ teaspoon ground turmeric

600ml (20fl oz) water

FOR THE TADKA

2 tablespoons sunflower oil

2 tablespoons ghee

1 teaspoon cumin seeds

10–12 fresh curry leaves

2.5-cm (1-in) piece of fresh root ginger, finely chopped

4 garlic cloves, finely chopped

1 onion, finely chopped

1 green chilli, finely chopped

1 tomato, finely chopped

1 teaspoon tamarind paste

1 tablespoon grated jaggery

handful of coriander leaves, finely chopped

100ml (3½fl oz) water

Put the lentils, salt, turmeric and measured water into a saucepan and bring to the boil. Cook over a medium heat for 10–12 minutes until lentils are soft and have begun to break up.

Meanwhile, prepare the tadka. Heat the oil and ghee in a large saucepan and add the cumin seeds. Cook over a medium-low heat for 1–2 minutes until they begin to sizzle. Now stir in the curry leaves and then, after a few seconds, the ginger and garlic. Cook over a low heat for 1 minute, then mix in the onion and chilli. Cook for 6–8 minutes until the onion turns golden.

Add the tomato to the saucepan, mix well and cook over a low heat for 5 minutes, then stir in the tamarind and jaggery and cook for 1 minute until the jaggery has melted. Mix in the coriander, then pour in the measured water and bring it to the boil. Add the tadka to the cooked lentils and mix well. Serve immediately.

A humble vegetable is transformed into something spectacular in this delicious salad. The spiced roasted cauliflower combines well with coriander, peanuts and a simple dressing. Enjoy this versatile salad warm, or let the cauliflower cool down and have it at room temperature. You can also serve the spiced cauliflower as a sabji (vegetable dish) alongside a main meal, or use it as a filling in wraps or sandwiches, or for pastry. The choice is yours.

Roasted cauliflower salad

SERVES 2

1 small cauliflower with leaves retained, cut into pieces

1 red onion, cut into chunks

¾ teaspoon salt

1 teaspoon chilli powder

1 teaspoon chaat masala

4 tablespoons rapeseed oil

2 tablespoons blanched peanuts

1 bunch of spring onions, roughly chopped

handful of coriander, finely chopped

FOR THE DRESSING

2 tablespoons olive oil

½ teaspoon cider vinegar

1 teaspoon honey

pinch of salt

pinch of freshly ground black pepper

Preheat the oven to 200°C (400°F), Gas Mark 6.

Put the cauliflower, cauliflower leaves and onion into a roasting tin, then sprinkle the salt, chilli powder and chaat masala on top. Drizzle over the oil. Mix it all up and ensure the veg is coated well in the oil and spices.

Roast the cauliflower and onion for 20 minutes, then remove the roasting tin from the oven and give the veg a good stir. Return the tin to the oven and roast for another 10–15 minutes until the vegetables are golden and cooked through.

Meanwhile, put the peanuts into a small frying pan and toast them over a low heat for 3–4 minutes until golden and crunchy. Now roughly crush the toasted peanuts using a pestle and mortar.

Put the roasted cauliflower and onion into a large bowl. Add the spring onions, coriander and crushed peanuts.

Combine the dressing ingredients in a small bowl and whisk together. Pour the dressing over the salad, toss well and serve immediately.

Who doesn't like an onion ring or two? This, though, is the ultimate version! These onion rings are stuffed with spiced potato and dipped in gram flour before frying to give them a light crispy coating. Serve with a lively chutney of your choice – any of the chutneys in this book will work well.

Potato-stuffed onion rings

SERVES 2

2 onions, cut into thin rings no thicker than 1cm (½in)

sunflower oil, for deep-frying

FOR THE FILLING

2 tablespoons sunflower oil

½ teaspoon mustard seeds

½ teaspoon salt

½ teaspoon ground turmeric

½ teaspoon chilli powder

½ teaspoon chaat masala

2 medium potatoes, boiled, peeled and mashed

FOR THE BATTER

100g (3½oz) gram flour

140–150ml (4¾–5fl oz) water

¼ teaspoon salt

½ teaspoon chaat masala

¼ teaspoon ground turmeric

¼ teaspoon chilli powder

First, make the filling. Heat the oil in a saucepan over a medium–low heat. Add the mustard seeds and cook for 1–2 minutes until they begin to sizzle. Stir in the salt and spices, quickly followed by the mashed potatoes. Mix well, then take the pan off the heat and set aside to allow the mixture to cool slightly.

Place the onion rings flat on your work surface and fill the centres with the potato mixture.

Mix the batter ingredients to a smooth batter in a bowl.

Heat the oil in a deep saucepan or deep-fat fryer to a cooking temperature of 170–180°C (340–350°F). (Maintain this temperature range throughout cooking.) Dip the stuffed onion rings into the batter one by one, coating them well, then carefully lower into the hot oil. You will need to fry them in batches to avoid overcrowding the pan. Cook for 1–2 minutes on each side until golden. Using a slotted spoon, transfer the onion rings to a plate lined with kitchen paper and leave to drain while you cook subsequent batches. Serve warm with your choice of chutney.

These delicious chicken wings are sticky, sweet and spicy all at once, and charred well to crisp up the edges. The curry is fragrant and light, forming a lovely sauce for the chicken. Resist the temptation to start eating the wings without the sauce as soon as they come out of the oven because, chances are, there won't be any wings left by the time the sauce is ready!

Sticky spicy chicken wings with tomato curry

SERVES 2

1kg (2lb 4oz) chicken wings

FOR THE MARINADE
2 teaspoons honey
3 teaspoons sunflower oil
½ teaspoon salt
½ teaspoon chilli powder
½ teaspoon garam masala
1 tablespoon tomato ketchup
4 garlic cloves, grated

Preheat the oven to 200°C (400°F), Gas Mark 6.

Put all the marinade ingredients into a large bowl and mix well. Add the chicken wings and mix with the marinade to ensure they are well coated. Spread the wings across a baking tin, then add to the tin any marinade that is left in the bowl. Roast the chicken for 50–55 minutes until cooked through and beautifully golden.

During the final 20 minutes or so of cooking time for the chicken, prepare the curry so that both elements are cooked at roughly the same time. Heat the oil and 1 tablespoon of the butter in a saucepan over a low heat. Once hot, add the cardamom and garlic and cook over a low heat for 1 minute until the garlic is lightly golden. Add the passata, cover the pan with a lid and cook over a low heat for 20 minutes until the tomato is cooked and slightly thickened.

FOR THE CURRY

1 tablespoon sunflower oil

2 tablespoons salted butter

4 cardamom pods

2 garlic cloves, finely chopped

200ml (7fl oz) passata

¼ teaspoon salt

¼ teaspoon chilli powder

¼ teaspoon garam masala

½ teaspoon honey

1 teaspoon dried fenugreek leaves (kasuri methi)

2 tablespoons double cream

Stir the salt, spices, honey and fenugreek leaves into the tomato and mix well. Next, mix in the cream, then top the curry with the remaining butter and let it melt in. If the sauce is too thick, add 1–2 tablespoons water and heat through.

Drizzle the curry on a serving plate. Spread the chicken wings on top and serve immediately.

See photograph overleaf.

Okra has a bad reputation as a slimy, stringy vegetable, which is grossly unfair because, when cooked properly, it has both a wonderful texture and flavour. For this dish I cook it with basic spices and tons of ginger and garlic, and to take it to the next level of amazing, I shallow-fry the okra briefly before adding it to the curry. Try it – you'll fall in love with this vegetable forever.

Okra masala

SERVES 2

6 tablespoons sunflower oil

400g (14oz) okra, cut into 1-cm (½-in) pieces

1 teaspoon cumin seeds

1 teaspoon carom seeds (ajwain)

1 green chilli, thinly sliced

1 onion, thinly sliced

2.5-cm (1-in) piece of fresh root ginger, julienned

4 garlic cloves, thinly sliced

1 tomato, thinly sliced

¾ teaspoon salt

¾ teaspoon chilli powder

1 teaspoon ground coriander

1 teaspoon garam masala

1 teaspoon amchur (mango powder)

Heat 4 tablespoons of the oil in a saucepan, then add the okra and fry over a high heat for 5–6 minutes until the pieces begin to change colour. Remove them from the pan with a slotted spoon and transfer to a plate lined with kitchen paper to drain the excess oil.

Return the saucepan to the heat and pour in the remaining 2 tablespoons oil. Now add the cumin and carom seeds and cook over a medium–low heat for 1–2 minutes until they begin to sizzle. Mix in the chilli, onion, ginger and garlic and cook over a medium–low heat for 5 minutes until softened. Now add the tomato, salt and spices and mix well.

Next, add the fried okra to the saucepan and mix well. Cover the pan with a lid and cook over a low heat for 10 minutes until the okra is cooked through and no longer slimy or stringy. Serve hot.

This recipe offers a great way to dress up some sea bass. Frying the fish within a spicy batter adds flavour and gives it a lovely crispy coating. Feel free to switch up the fish for a change – cod or salmon are just a couple of varieties that work well.

Fish fry

SERVES 2

1 sea bass, roughly 500g (1lb 2oz), cleaned, gutted and cut into 1-cm (½-in) thick slices

½ teaspoon salt

½ teaspoon ground turmeric

1 tablespoon lemon juice

sunflower oil, for deep-frying

FOR THE BATTER

30g (1oz) cornflour

50g (1¾oz) gram flour

2.5-cm (1-in) piece of fresh root ginger, grated

¼ teaspoon salt

½ teaspoon chilli powder

½ teaspoon carom seeds (ajwain)

1 egg, lightly whisked

100ml (3½fl oz) water

Put the fish into a non-reactive bowl, sprinkle the salt and turmeric on top, then drizzle over the lemon juice. Now rub these additions all over the fish pieces. Cover the bowl and leave to rest for 10 minutes.

Meanwhile, prepare the batter. Whisk all the batter ingredients together in a bowl until smooth.

Heat the oil in a deep saucepan or deep-fat fryer to a cooking temperature of 160–170°C (325–340°F). (Maintain this temperature range throughout cooking.)

Working with 1 piece at a time, dip the pieces of fish into the batter, then carefully lower them into the hot oil. Cook for 2 minutes on each side until golden and cooked. Using a slotted spoon, transfer each fish piece to a plate lined with kitchen paper and leave to drain while you cook subsequent pieces. Serve immediately once all the pieces are cooked.

I love aubergine – it has such an amazing flavour if you cook it properly, and this delicious all-in-one meal is the perfect example of well-prepared aubergine combined with the usual basic spices. The addition of curry leaves, tamarind and fresh coconut add lovely tone and texture. If you have leftover rice, it's the perfect excuse for making this stunning dish.

Aubergine coconut rice

SERVES 2

4 tablespoons sunflower oil

1 teaspoon mustard seeds

1 onion, thinly sliced

10–12 fresh curry leaves

1 medium potato, peeled and cut into 2.5-cm (1-in) dice

1 aubergine, cut into 2.5-cm (1-in) dice

1 teaspoon salt

1 teaspoon chilli powder

1 teaspoon garam masala

2 teaspoons ground coriander

1 teaspoon tamarind paste

1 teaspoon soft brown sugar

80g (2¾oz) grated fresh coconut

400g (14oz) cooked basmati rice

Heat the oil in a saucepan over a medium–low heat and add the mustard seeds. Cook for 1–2 minutes until they begin to pop, then add the onion and curry leaves and cook over a medium heat for 5 minutes until the onion begins to colour.

Add the potato and aubergine to the pan and cook over a high heat for 2 minutes until they begin to colour. Now cover the pan with a lid, reduce the heat to low and cook for 12 minutes or until the potato and aubergine are cooked through.

Next, stir in the salt and spices, the tamarind, sugar and the grated coconut flesh and cook over a low heat for a couple of minutes until everything is mixed well. Then stir in the cooked rice and cook over a high heat for 5 minutes, stirring continuously, until the rice is completely heated through. Serve immediately.

Parathas are simply the best. I remember taking parathas of all sorts for packed lunches at school, on train journeys, for picnics and having them whenever my mum needed to put a meal together quickly. Including spinach in the dough adds both flavour and texture to this tasty version – enjoy it with just some butter, a little chutney or with any curry.

Spinach onion paratha

MAKES 4

150g (5½oz) chapati flour, plus extra for dusting

½ teaspoon salt

½ teaspoon chilli powder

½ teaspoon chaat masala

1 green chilli, finely chopped

100g (3½oz) spinach leaves, finely chopped

handful of coriander leaves, finely chopped

approximately 4 tablespoons water

1 teaspoon ghee, plus extra for cooking

Coriander Yogurt Chutney (see page 54), to serve (optional)

Put the flour, salt, spices and the chopped fresh ingredients into a mixing bowl and mix to combine. Now slowly add just enough of the measured water (or more, if necessary) to bring the mixture together into a soft dough. Knead the dough for 2 minutes.

Divide the dough into 4 equal portions. Roll out each portion on a lightly floured surface into a thin circle with a diameter of roughly 10cm (4in). Brush ghee generously across the top surface. Fold the circle in half, then fold the semicircle you've just created in half to form a triangle. Press it gently and roll it until the triangle measures roughly 15–18cm (6–7in).

Heat a frying pan and, once hot, cook 1 paratha over a medium heat for 1 minute on each side until golden. Now drizzle 1 tablespoon ghee over the top surface and turn it over to cook that side again for 1 minute until crispy. Meanwhile, drizzle 1 tablespoon ghee over the surface now facing up. Once the underside is crispy, flip the paratha over and cook for another minute until both sides are crispy. Transfer to a plate and repeat the process to cook the remaining paratha. Serve with my Coriander Yogurt Chutney, if liked.

When you roast garlic slowly in the oven, the flavour becomes delicate and sweet – very different to pungent raw garlic. And if you combine roasted garlic with yogurt, dill and spices, you have the most delicious raita. I suggest you roast the garlic while your oven is already on for cooking something, to conserve energy (cooking just one garlic bulb in the oven is not the wisest move). It's ok if you prepare the garlic a few days in advance and store it in an airtight container in the refrigerator until you need it.

Roasted garlic raita

SERVES 2

1 small garlic bulb

1 tablespoon olive oil

2 pinches of salt

2 pinches of freshly ground black pepper

100ml (3½fl oz) natural yogurt

pinch of ground cumin

handful of dill, roughly chopped

Preheat the oven to 180°C (350°F), Gas Mark 4.

Cut the garlic bulb in half crossways and place it on a piece of kitchen foil. Drizzle over the oil, then sprinkle 1 pinch each of salt and pepper on top. Bunch up the foil to enclose the garlic and bake for 40–45 minutes until the garlic is very soft. Set aside until cool enough to handle.

Whisk the yogurt with the remaining salt and pepper, the ground cumin and the dill.

Using your fingers, squeeze the roasted garlic cloves out of the skins into a small bowl, then mash them with a fork. Stir the mashed garlic into the yogurt mixture and serve.

This spicy chutney has a pleasing crunch to it. The chana dal adds that textured base, while the tamarind paste gives it a slight tang that combines well with the light sweetness and the chilli heat. Serve this alongside any meal to make it a little more exciting.

Chana dal chutney

SERVES 2

2 tablespoons sunflower oil

100g (3½oz) chana dal (split yellow peas)

6 dried red chillies

100ml (3½fl oz) boiling water

70g (2½oz) grated fresh coconut

½ teaspoon salt

1 teaspoon soft brown sugar

1 teaspoon tamarind paste

FOR THE TADKA

1 teaspoon sunflower oil

1 teaspoon mustard seeds

10 fresh curry leaves

Heat the oil in a saucepan, then add the chana dal and dried red chillies and cook over a low heat for 2 minutes until the dal is evenly coated in the oil. Now stir in the measured boiling water, cover the pan with a lid and cook over a low heat for 15 minutes until the dal begins to soften on the outside.

Now add the coconut, salt, sugar and tamarind paste to the pan, then take it off the heat. Using a stick blender, blitz the mixture to a paste, then transfer it to a serving bowl.

To make the tadka, heat the oil in a small saucepan over a medium–low heat. Add the mustard seeds and curry leaves and let them sizzle for 1–2 minutes. Now pour the mixture evenly across the surface of the chutney and serve.

Although this dessert is easy and quick to prepare, its flavour is amazing. If I make a couple of these for my kids, they are demolished in seconds! I love using this specific combination of ingredients, but you can swap out the Biscoff biscuits and spread for any digestives or spread of your choice. Chocolate spread and caramel sauce are both great substitutes.

Biscoff cheesecake delight

SERVES 2

50g (1¾oz) Lotus Biscoff biscuits (or any digestive biscuits)

20g (¾oz) salted butter, melted

200g (7oz) cream cheese

2 tablespoons icing sugar

50ml (2fl oz) double cream

2 tablespoons smooth Lotus Biscoff spread

TO SERVE

1 tablespoon smooth Lotus Biscoff spread

2 tablespoons water

2 Lotus Biscoff biscuits (or any digestive biscuits), crushed

Put the biscuits into a bowl and crush them to a fine crumb with the end of a rolling pin. Now mix in the melted butter. Divide the mixture into 2 equal portions and transfer these to cocktail glasses or small bowls. Refrigerate for 15 minutes to set.

Put the cream cheese and icing sugar into a bowl and beat together with a wooden spoon until smooth. Now add the double cream and mix together. Next, fold in the Lotus Biscoff spread, but ensure it is not completely mixed in – you want to leave pockets of spread in the sweet cream cheese mixture for bursts of flavour.

Spoon the sweet cream cheese mixture over the biscuit bases and smooth out the tops. Refrigerate for a couple of hours or overnight to set.

When you're ready to serve, put the Lotus Biscoff spread and measured water into a small bowl and stir together to loosen the spread. Drizzle the mixture across the tops of the puddings as well as the insides of the serving glasses or bowls, then sprinkle the crushed biscuits on top. Serve immediately.

Being a working mum, I know it's vital to have recipes up your sleeve for delicious meals that can be cooked in a flash. Midweek after work, I need to be able to cook meals quickly, but don't want to compromise on flavour, as I outline in my book *Chetna's 30 Minute Indian*, which is full of quick and easy recipes. There is so much satisfaction in being able to prepare a dish speedily that is received with joy. If you want to make a special feast but don't have much time, look no further than this chapter. I have packed it with recipes for quick dishes that everyone will love. The fresh Dal with Mango and the Ultimate Potato Sabji is a match made in heaven and my absolute favourite meal combo. The Spicy Ginger-garlic Chicken is sublime with the Peanut, Coriander and Lemon Rice, and the Sweetcorn Raita will complement anything. The Prawn Coconut Curry is dreamy with the Quick Naan and some Cauliflower Masala. My kids love the Onion Yogurt Paneer, which goes very well with the rice or naan. However, all the dishes in this chapter go really well with each other, so if you have a little more time and something to celebrate, cook them all to serve together! The Almond Halwa is a feast by itself, as it is wonderfully rich and absolutely delicious – the perfect sweet ending to a wonderful meal.

Fast feasts

Spicy ginger-garlic chicken

Dal with mango

Cauliflower masala

Onion yogurt paneer

Prawn coconut curry

Moong dal salad

Ultimate potato sabji

Peanut, coriander and lemon rice

Sweetcorn raita

Quick naan

Almond halwa

The marinade used in this dish is magic! It gives chicken pieces the delicious flavour of a lovely combination of spices, with the perfect hint of sourness from the lemon juice and a pleasing crisp texture from the rice flour. Every time I make this dish it disappears in seconds, so now I always make double the quantity.

Spicy ginger-garlic chicken

SERVES 4

4 boneless, skinless chicken thighs, cut into quarters

4 tablespoons rapeseed oil

3 green chillies, halved lengthways and fried, to garnish (optional)

FOR THE MARINADE

2 tablespoons rapeseed oil

1 tablespoon lemon juice

2 tablespoons rice flour

1 teaspoon chilli powder

1 teaspoon salt

1 teaspoon ground cumin

1 teaspoon garam masala

2 garlic cloves, grated

1-cm (½-in) piece of fresh root ginger, grated

Put all the marinade ingredients into a non-reactive bowl and mix well. Add the chicken pieces and mix to coat them in the marinade.

Heat the oil in a frying pan over a medium heat. Add the chicken pieces and cook for 5 minutes on each side until deep golden and crispy and cooked through. Using a slotted spoon, transfer the chicken pieces to a plate lined with kitchen paper to drain, then serve immediately, garnished with the fried green chillies, if liked.

There are many types of lentils and they all taste so different. If you want a quick lentil dish, use red lentils, also known as masoor dal, as they take the least amount of time to cook. In just 15 minutes, they are cooked and super-soft. The flavour of the dal and mango in this dish is exceptional, and the tadka just shines through.

Dal with mango

SERVES 4

2 tablespoons sunflower oil

1 teaspoon cumin seeds

10 fresh curry leaves

2.5-cm (1-in) piece of fresh root ginger, grated

1 red onion, roughly chopped

2 tomatoes, roughly chopped

1 green underripe mango, peeled, stoned and grated

1 teaspoon salt

1 teaspoon ground turmeric

1 teaspoon chilli powder

1 teaspoon ground coriander

300g (10½oz) masoor dal (red lentils)

1.2 litres (2 pints) boiling water

FOR THE TADKA

2 tablespoons ghee

4 garlic cloves, thinly sliced

2 green chillies, thinly sliced

Heat the oil in a saucepan over a medium–low heat. Add the cumin seeds and cook for a few seconds until they begin to pop, then mix in the curry leaves, followed by the ginger. Allow these to sizzle for a few seconds, then stir in the onion. Cook over a medium–low heat for 6–8 minutes until lightly golden.

Now mix the tomatoes and mango into the onion and cook for 2 minutes, then add the salt and spices and mix well. Next, stir in the lentils, then the measured boiling water. Cover the pan with a lid and cook the dal over a low heat for 15 minutes until the lentils are soft and cooked through.

To make the tadka, heat the ghee in a small pan over a medium–low heat, then stir in the garlic and chillies. Allow the mixture to sizzle for a few seconds, then pour it over the cooked lentils to serve.

This is a stunning veggie dish, yet it's easy to make and ready in a flash! Cauliflower is one of my favourite vegetables. It can be cooked in so many ways and lends itself to all sorts of spicing. For this recipe I add all the flavours from my spice box as well as some chilli-garlic sauce for extra depth. You can use any shop-bought chilli-garlic sauce, but if you don't have any, substitute harissa or a chilli-tomato sauce – either works beautifully.

Cauliflower masala

SERVES 4

2 tablespoons sunflower oil

1 teaspoon fennel seeds

1 teaspoon cumin seeds

3 onions, thinly sliced

2.5-cm (1-in) piece of fresh root ginger, finely chopped

4 garlic cloves, finely chopped

1 green chilli, finely chopped

2 tomatoes, thinly sliced

1 teaspoon salt

1 teaspoon ground turmeric

2 teaspoons ground coriander

1 teaspoon garam masala

1 teaspoon chilli powder

1 tablespoon shop-bought chilli-garlic sauce

1 cauliflower, cut into florets

8–10 mint leaves, finely chopped

Heat the sunflower oil in a saucepan over a medium–low heat. Add the fennel and cumin seeds and cook for 1–2 minutes until they begin to sizzle. Stir in the onions and cook over a medium–low heat for 8–10 minutes until golden.

Add the ginger, garlic and chilli to the saucepan, stir well and cook for 1 minute. Add the tomatoes and mix well. Stir the salt and spices in, then add the chilli-garlic sauce.

Finally, add the cauliflower to the saucepan and mix well, then cover the pan with a lid and cook over a medium–low heat for 10–12 minutes until the florets are softened and cooked through. Take the pan off the heat, sprinkle over the mint and serve immediately.

It's unusual to have no tomatoes in a curry, but this paneer curry, made with yogurt and fried onions, is creamy and quite gentle, yet aromatic and deeply flavourful.

Onion yogurt paneer

SERVES 4

100ml (3½fl oz) sunflower oil

4 onions, thinly sliced

2.5-cm (1-in) piece of fresh root ginger, cut into chunks

6 garlic cloves, cut into chunks

200ml (7fl oz) water

2 bay leaves

4 cardamom pods

4 cloves

1 cinnamon stick

150ml (¼ pint) natural yogurt

1 teaspoon salt

1 teaspoon chilli powder

1 teaspoon garam masala

1 teaspoon ground coriander

1 teaspoon ground cumin

450g (1lb) paneer, cut into 2.5-cm (1-in) cubes

2 tablespoons double cream

Heat the oil in a saucepan, then add the onions and cook over a medium heat for 10–12 minutes until golden. Now stir in the ginger and garlic and cook for 2 minutes more.

Spoon the onion mixture into a heatproof sieve, place this over a pan or heatproof bowl and set aside for 5 minutes to allow any excess oil to drain out of the onions. Reserve the oil and transfer the onion mixture to a blender, add half the measured water and blitz to a smooth purée.

Put 1 tablespoon of the reserved oil back into the pan you used to cook the onions, then add the bay leaves and whole spices. Mix in the onion purée and cook over a low heat for 5 minutes until the mixture is heated through.

Take the pan off the heat, pour in the yogurt and remaining measured water and stir for 1 minute. Now return the pan to the hob and cook the mixture over a low heat for 5 minutes until it thickens slightly.

Stir the salt and ground spices into the pan and cook for 1 minute, then mix in the paneer. Cook over a low heat for another 5 minutes to cook the paneer and allow it to take on all the flavours of the masala. Stir in the cream and serve immediately.

If you've got just a handful of spices, some fresh king prawns and roughly 10 minutes, you can have this simple yet sublime curry! Enjoy it on a pile of piping-hot rice.

Prawn coconut curry

SERVES 4

2 tablespoons rapeseed oil

2 bay leaves

4 cloves

4 cardamom pods

1 cinnamon stick

2 onions, finely chopped

2.5-cm (1-in) piece of fresh root ginger, finely chopped

½ teaspoon ground turmeric

1 teaspoon chilli powder

½ teaspoon salt

16 raw king prawns, peeled and deveined, tails left intact

400ml (14fl oz) can of coconut milk

Heat the oil in a saucepan over a medium–low heat. Add the bay leaves, cloves, cardamom and cinnamon and cook over a medium heat for 1–2 minutes until they begin to sizzle. Stir in the onions and ginger and cook for 6–8 minutes until slightly golden. Now add the turmeric, chilli powder and salt and mix well.

Next, stir in the prawns and cook over a high heat for 1 minute. Now pour in the coconut milk, bring it to the boil and cook over a high heat for 2 minutes until the prawns have turned pink and are done. Serve immediately.

Inspired by kosambari, a South Indian dish, this salad is amazingly healthy and has a lovely collection of flavours and textures going on. The potatoes add substance and bite, the lentils bring in a delightful crunchiness and a hint of chilli works well with the sweetness of the coconut. A fragrant curry leaf tadka provides the perfect dressing and brings the whole thing together.

Moong dal salad

SERVES 4–6

100g (3½oz) moong dal (split mung beans)

1 medium potato, boiled, peeled and finely chopped

1 cucumber, finely chopped

handful of coriander leaves, finely chopped

1 green chilli, finely chopped

3 tablespoons grated fresh coconut

¼ teaspoon salt

2 tablespoons lemon juice

FOR THE TADKA

2 tablespoons rapeseed oil

1 teaspoon mustard seeds

8–10 fresh curry leaves

Soak the lentils in boiling water for 2 hours. Once the soaking time has elapsed, drain the lentils and transfer them to a bowl. Add the remaining main ingredients and mix well.

To make the tadka, heat the oil in a small pan over a medium–low heat. Add the mustard seeds and curry leaves and let them sizzle for a few seconds, then take the pan off the heat. Pour the tadka over the salad, mix well and serve immediately.

At first I was having trouble finding the right name for this sabji (vegetable dish). It is spicy, moreishly sour and the most delicious, quick and flavourful potato dish you will ever make. Then the word 'ultimate' came to mind, because that's what it is – simply the best potato sabji!

Ultimate potato sabji

SERVES 4

50ml (2fl oz) rapeseed oil

pinch of asafoetida

1 teaspoon cumin seeds

1 onion, finely chopped

2.5-cm (1-in) piece of fresh root ginger, finely chopped

4 garlic cloves, finely chopped

1 green chilli, finely chopped

4 medium potatoes, peeled and cut into 2.5-cm (1-in) dice

½ teaspoon salt

½ teaspoon ground turmeric

½ teaspoon chaat masala

1 teaspoon chilli powder

1 teaspoon garam masala

1 teaspoon amchur (mango powder)

handful of coriander leaves, finely chopped

Heat the oil in a saucepan over a medium–low heat. Add the asafoetida and cumin and let the mixture sizzle for a few seconds, then stir in the onion and cook for 4–5 minutes until softened.

Add the ginger, garlic and chilli to the pan, mix well and continue to cook over a medium–low heat for 1 minute. Next, stir in the potatoes and cook over a high heat for 1 minute. Now cover the pan with a lid and cook over a low heat for 10–12 minutes until the potatoes are cooked through and soft.

Add the salt and spices to the pan with the coriander, mix well and cook over a high heat for 1 minute more, then serve immediately.

This simple peanut-lemon rice with lots of coriander and curry leaves is seriously delicious. Because it is ready within minutes, it's perfect for when you need a substantial snack (have it with your favourite chutney), but it also makes a lovely accompaniment to any curry.

Peanut, coriander and lemon rice

SERVES 4

2 tablespoons groundnut oil

60g (2¼oz) blanched peanuts

1 teaspoon mustard seeds

12–14 fresh curry leaves

1 onion, thinly sliced

2 green chillies, thinly sliced

handful of coriander leaves, roughly chopped

1 teaspoon salt

1 teaspoon chilli powder

1 teaspoon ground turmeric

1 teaspoon ground cumin

300g (10½oz) basmati rice, washed and drained

grated zest and juice of 2 lemons

600ml (20fl oz) boiling water

Heat the oil in a saucepan, then add the peanuts. Cook over a medium–low heat for 2 minutes until golden. Stir in the mustard seeds and curry leaves and let them sizzle for a few seconds, then mix in the onion and chillies. Cook for 5 minutes until they have softened.

Next, add the coriander, salt and spices to the pan and mix well. Now add the rice and stir until all the rice is coated well. Mix in the lemon zest and measured boiling water, cover the pan with a lid and cook over a low heat for 10 minutes until the rice is almost cooked.

Lift off the lid, pour in the lemon juice evenly across the top of the rice, then replace the lid and cook over a low heat for 5 minutes until the rice is fully cooked. Leave to rest without taking the lid off for 10 minutes before serving.

Fresh corn, just cut off the cob, is so sweet, juicy and delicious. And if you cook it in butter and chaat masala you give it a lovely little tang that goes well with a flavoured yogurt.

Sweetcorn raita

SERVES 4

FOR THE CORN

2 corn on the cob (or 200g/ 7oz frozen sweetcorn kernels)

1 teaspoon sunflower oil

1 teaspoon salted butter

1 green chilli, finely chopped

pinch of salt

¼ teaspoon chaat masala

FOR THE SPICED YOGURT

200ml (7fl oz) natural yogurt

pinch of salt

pinch of freshly ground black pepper

¼ teaspoon ground cumin

If using corn cobs, remove the husks and cut off all the corn kernels from the cobs using a sharp knife.

Heat the oil and butter in a frying pan, add the corn and chilli and cook over a low heat for 4–5 minutes until the corn becomes golden. Now add the salt and chaat masala and mix well. Take the pan off the heat and set aside to allow the cooked corn to cool down.

To make the spiced yogurt, put all the ingredients into a bowl and whisk until well combined. Spread the mixture across a serving plate.

Once the corn has cooled, sprinkle it over the spiced yogurt to serve.

This is a super-simple and quick naan recipe. Adding baking powder and yogurt to the dough creates fluffy, pillowy naan breads that are ready in minutes. Once made, you can top the naan with garlic, chilli and coriander if you like.

Quick naan

MAKES 4

220g (7¾oz) self-raising flour, plus extra for dusting

¼ teaspoon salt

¼ teaspoon chilli flakes

¼ teaspoon nigella seeds

200ml (7fl oz) natural yogurt

salted butter or ghee, to serve

Mix the flour, salt, chilli flakes and nigella seeds in a mixing bowl. Add the yogurt and mix well with your hands to form a dough. The dough may be slightly sticky at first, but continue to knead it for 2–3 minutes until it becomes a little smoother. Leave the dough in the bowl, cover the bowl with a clean tea towel and let the dough rest for 5 minutes.

Heat a frying pan or griddle pan over a medium heat. Divide the dough into 4 equal portions. Dust your work surface with a little flour, then roll out each dough portion into a circle with a diameter of 13–15cm (5–6in). Cook in the hot pan for 1 minute on each side until golden.

Once cooked, brush each naan with butter or ghee and serve nice and hot.

Halwa is one of the easiest Indian desserts to cook, and the ingredients are versatile – you can use nuts, semolina, lentils or flour. The almond version is usually made by soaking the whole nuts overnight, then peeling them, drying them and grinding them to a powder. I make the process quicker and easier by using ready-ground almonds – much less work for all the taste! Use ghee to cook this dish if you can – the flavours and oils released are delicious.

Almond halwa

SERVES 4

100g (3½oz) unsalted butter or ghee

140g (5oz) ground almonds

140ml (4¾fl oz) milk

¼ teaspoon ground cardamom

pinch of saffron threads

40g (1½oz) golden caster sugar

handful of pistachio nuts, crushed

Heat the butter or ghee in a saucepan over a medium heat. Once it begins to bubble and sizzle, add the ground almonds and reduce the heat to low. Cook for 12–14 minutes, stirring every 2 minutes, until the mixture turns a deep golden colour.

Meanwhile, pour the milk into a jug, add the cardamom and saffron and stir well to combine. Set aside.

Add the sugar to the almond mixture in the pan and mix well. Continue to cook over a low heat for 2 minutes, stirring continuously to encourage the sugar to dissolve. Once the sugar has dissolved, slowly pour in the spiced milk, stirring continuously until the milk is incorporated. Now cook for 3–4 minutes until the mixture thickens. Take the pan off the heat, then sprinkle the crushed pistachios on top. Serve warm.

Summer is the time to be outdoors, feeling the grass under your feet, sitting in the dappled shade beneath the trees and enjoying delicious meals cooked on the barbecue. This chapter showcases some of my favourite barbecue dishes. I'm definitely a fair-weather barbecuing type – you won't find me standing in front of the grill in the rain! If you're like me, bear in mind that the dishes I cook here on the grill can also be made in the oven or on the hob. So should there be an unexpected squall on the day of your planned gathering, or if you have a sudden craving for one of these dishes during deepest, darkest midwinter, there's nothing to stop you from enjoying them. The Masala Spatchcock Chicken is amazing when coal-smoked, but its marinade is so full of flavour, you'll end up making the oven-cooked version out of barbecue season. The Spicy King Prawns are stunning with some Roast Tomato Raita or the Red Onion Salad. Try the Paneer Skewers served with some Naan and Tomato and Peanut Chutney. The Tamarind Potatoes make a fantastic side dish and are great to snack on, too. Serve this feast with Skikanji, the perfect drink to refresh the palate after a big barbecue. Then wrap it all up with the stunning Caramelized Walnut and Coffee Pavlova to finish on the perfect sweet note.

Barbecue

Paneer skewers

Masala spatchcock chicken

Spicy king prawns

Tamarind potatoes

Red onion salad

Garlic chilli corn

Naan on the barbecue

Tomato and peanut chutney

Roast tomato raita

Caramelized walnut and coffee pavlova

Skikanji

Being a great flavour carrier, paneer turns up in all sorts of Indian feasts. In this recipe, its plainness is the perfect base for this fantastic blend of spices, which is mixed with yogurt and gram flour to keep the paneer moist and sticky.

Paneer skewers

SERVES 4

1 red onion, cut into chunks

1 red pepper, cored, deseeded and cut into chunks

1 green pepper, cored, deseeded and cut into chunks

225g (8oz) paneer, cubed

sunflower oil, for brushing

lemon wedges, for squeezing over

Naan (see page 128), to serve (optional)

FOR THE MARINADE

3 tablespoons gram flour

150ml (¼ pint) natural yogurt

½ teaspoon salt

1 teaspoon amchur (mango powder)

1 teaspoon garam masala

½ teaspoon ground turmeric

1 teaspoon chilli powder

TO FINISH

2 tablespoons ghee

1 teaspoon chilli flakes

¼ teaspoon chaat masala

First, soak 12 miniature wooden skewers in water for 30 minutes (this stops them burning). Next, make the marinade. Toast the gram flour in a pan over a low heat for 2 minutes until it begins to change colour. Transfer the toasted flour to a bowl with the remaining marinade ingredients and mix well.

Light the barbecue. While waiting for the coals to be ready for cooking, prepare the skewers. Put the onion, peppers and paneer into the marinade and gently coat them with the mix. Spear the vegetable and paneer pieces onto the skewers and brush them with oil.

Place the skewers on the barbecue grill and cook for 6–8 minutes, turning them occasionally so that the vegetable chunks and paneer cubes are charred all over. When they are done, place them on a serving plate. (Alternatively, cook the unskewered marinated vegetables and paneer in a frying pan in some oil for 4–5 minutes until golden.)

To finish, melt the ghee in a small pan over a low heat, then take it off the heat. Stir in the chilli flakes and chaat masala, then pour the mixture over the skewers and serve immediately with lemon wedges for squeezing over and naan on the side, if liked.

All the basic ground spices from your spice cupboard go into this beautifully flavoured chicken. I like to use spatchcock chicken on the barbecue, as it cooks evenly and faster than a whole chicken. You could use this marinade for a whole chicken, or for chicken pieces, too – just remember that you will need to adjust the cooking times accordingly (you'll need more time for a whole chicken, and less time for chicken pieces).

Masala spatchcock chicken

SERVES 4

1 spatchcock chicken, around 1–1.5kg (2lb 4oz–3lb 5oz)

FOR THE MARINADE

2.5-cm (1-in) piece of fresh root ginger, peeled and grated

6 garlic cloves, grated

2 teaspoons chilli powder

1 teaspoon ground turmeric

2 teaspoons salt

2 teaspoons garam masala

½ teaspoon freshly ground black pepper

1 teaspoon ground cumin

2 teaspoons ground coriander

2 tablespoons lemon juice

1 tablespoon rapeseed oil

Mix all the marinade ingredients together in a non-reactive bowl. Place the chicken in a baking tin, then spread the marinade all over the chicken. Make sure you cover both the top and underside of the chicken. Cover with kitchen foil and leave to marinate for an hour or as long as you can in the refrigerator – preferably overnight.

Light up the barbecue and, when it is ready, place the chicken on the barbecue grill. Cover and leave to cook for 25 minutes before turning it over. Cook for a further 25 minutes or until done (check by inserting a knife into the thigh – if the juices run clear, then the chicken is cooked).

Once cooked, transfer the chicken to a serving plate, cover with kitchen foil and leave to rest for 10 minutes before serving.

Alternatively, cook the marinated spatchcock chicken in the oven preheated to 200°C (400°F), Gas Mark 6 for 50–60 minutes or until done.

It's the simple ingredients that bring so much joy to this prawn dish and, when cooked on a barbecue, the flavour deepens with all the smokiness added to it.

Spicy king prawns

SERVES 4

12 raw king prawns

grilled lemon halves, for squeezing over

FOR THE MARINADE

2 tablespoons rapeseed oil

handful of coriander leaves, finely chopped

big pinch of salt

¼ teaspoon freshly ground black pepper

¼ teaspoon pomegranate powder

¼ teaspoon chilli powder

1 red chilli, finely chopped

To prepare the prawns, peel off the shells, keeping the heads and tails intact, and devein. (If you prefer, you can remove the heads and tails, too, but retaining them makes cooking on the barbecue much easier.)

Put all the marinade ingredients into a bowl and mix well. Place the prawns in the marinade, cover the bowl and leave them to marinate for 30–60 minutes in the refrigerator.

Light the barbecue. Once the coals are ready for cooking, place the prawns on the barbecue grill. (If you removed the heads and tails, you might want to skewer the prawns to make it easier to handle them.) Cook for roughly 2 minutes on each side until cooked through. (Alternatively, cook the prawns in a frying pan over a medium heat for roughly 2 minutes on each side.) Serve with grilled lemon halves for squeezing over.

The Tamarind Jaggery Chutney gives these potatoes a lovely sweet and sour flavour. Combine that with some garlic and chilli, and this dish is on fire!

Tamarind potatoes

SERVES 2

2 medium potatoes, cut into 7.5mm (⅜-in) thick slices

sea salt

chopped coriander, to garnish

FOR THE MARINADE

2 tablespoons rapeseed oil, plus extra for brushing

¼ teaspoon salt

¼ teaspoon chilli powder

¼ teaspoon garlic granules

2 tablespoons Tamarind Jaggery Chutney (see page 53)

Place the potato slices in a saucepan and cover with water. Bring to the boil and cook for 3–4 minutes until the potatoes just begin to soften. Drain the potatoes and set aside to cool slightly.

Put all the marinade ingredients into a bowl and mix well. Add the potatoes to the bowl and carefully coat them in the mixture.

Light the barbecue. When the coals are ready for cooking, place the potatoes on the barbecue grill. Cook for 3–4 minutes on each side until golden and cooked through. You might need to brush them with more oil if they become too sticky, so have some handy at the side of the barbecue. (You can also cook the potatoes in a frying pan over a medium heat for the same amount of time.) Serve garnished with chopped coriander and sprinkled with sea salt.

A staple accompaniment to Indian dishes, this crunchy, spicy salad works well with any feast. Red onions will give your feast table a beautiful pop of colour, but you can substitute any type of onion, or even small or banana shallots.

Red onion salad

SERVES 4

½ teaspoon chilli powder

½ teaspoon chaat masala

pinch of salt

pinch of freshly ground black pepper

juice of 1 lime

handful of coriander leaves, finely chopped

2 red onions, cut into thin rings

Combine all the ingredients, except the onions, in a bowl, then add the onions. Mix it all up well and serve.

One of my favourite memories is of devouring freshly cooked corn on the cob while standing in the rain in a Mumbai monsoon. You can buy it from street stalls – little carts in which the vendors begin to cook the corn as you order it, working under an umbrella during the seasonal rains. Once cooked, they cover the corn with a basic mixture of salt, chilli and lemon juice. For this recipe, I've added a few more flavours that blend beautifully with the charred corn.

Garlic chilli corn

SERVES 2

2 whole corns on the cob

1 tablespoon salted butter

1 green chilli, finely chopped

1 garlic clove, grated

pinch of salt

pinch of kala namak
(black salt)

¼ teaspoon chaat masala

Light the barbecue.

Peel back the husks of each cob and tie them together with one of the leaves. Once the coals are ready for cooking, place the cobs on the barbecue grill and cook for 5–10 minutes, turning frequently, until charred all over.

Meanwhile, combine the butter with the remaining ingredients in a small bowl and mix well. Brush the seasoned butter over the cooked corn and serve.

Naan provides the perfect carrier for the delicious food being cooked on the barbecue, be it meat or vegetables, and it is great with just some salad or raita, too. Easy to make, these breads are wonderfully soft, yet hardy enough to be fully loaded.

Naan on the barbecue

MAKES 8

FOR THE DOUGH

400g (14oz) plain flour, plus extra for dusting

1 teaspoon salt

1 teaspoon granulated sugar

2 teaspoons fast-action dried yeast

130ml (4¼fl oz) natural yogurt

140ml (4¾fl oz) water

oil, for greasing

FOR BRUSHING

2 garlic cloves, grated

handful of coriander leaves, finely chopped

2 tablespoons salted butter, melted

Put the flour, salt, sugar and yeast into a bowl and mix together. Now mix in the yogurt, then slowly stir in the measured water a little at a time. Bring the mixture together to form a soft dough. Knead for 5 minutes, then place the dough in a lightly oiled bowl. Cover with a clean tea towel and leave to prove for 1–2 hours.

Light the barbecue. Divide the dough into 8 equal portions, cover with the tea towel and leave to prove while waiting for the coals to be ready for cooking.

Roll out each dough portion on a lightly floured surface into an oval shape and place it directly on the barbecue grill. Now cook for 1–2 minutes until it begins to puff up and becomes golden. Turn it over and cook on the other side for 1–2 minutes.

In a small bowl, mix together the garlic, coriander and butter. Brush this over the piping-hot naan and serve.

You might be surprised by this unusual match, but cooked tomatoes and peanuts, blended together with some carefully selected spices, make a delicious and moreish chutney that goes well with any of my barbecue dishes. Serve it with the Spicy King Prawns (see page 120) or the Paneer Skewers (see page 116), the Tamarind Potatoes (see page 123) or the Masala Spatchcock Chicken (see page 119). It's also amazing with crisps or tortillas.

Tomato and peanut chutney

4 tablespoons blanched peanuts

3 tablespoons rapeseed oil

1 teaspoon cumin seeds

2.5-cm (1-in) piece of fresh root ginger, peeled and roughly chopped

1 onion, roughly chopped

4 tomatoes, roughly chopped

2 green chillies, roughly chopped

3 tablespoons water, plus extra for blending as necessary

½ teaspoon salt

1 teaspoon soft brown sugar

Toast the peanuts in a frying pan over a medium heat for 3–4 minutes until lightly golden. Transfer to a bowl and set aside.

Heat the oil in the same pan over a medium heat, then add the cumin seeds. Cook for a few seconds until they begin to sizzle, then add the ginger, onion, tomatoes and chillies. Cook over a medium heat for 10 minutes, then stir in the measured water and cook for another 20 minutes until everything is mushy and soft.

Add 3 tablespoons of the peanuts to the pan along with the salt and brown sugar and mix. Transfer the mixture to the bowl of a blender and blitz it to a purée, adding a tablespoon of water, if necessary, to help you blend the mixture.

Transfer the chutney to a serving bowl. Chop the remaining peanuts and sprinkle on top to serve.

There are so many layers of flavours in this simple dish of charred tomatoes sitting on a bed of spiced thickened yogurt, finished with a simple tadka. The sum is truly greater than the parts.

Roast tomato raita

SERVES 4

500ml (18fl oz) natural yogurt

8 tomatoes, halved

1 tablespoon sunflower oil, for brushing

½ teaspoon salt

½ teaspoon chilli powder

FOR THE TADKA

2 tablespoons ghee

1 teaspoon mustard seeds

10 fresh curry leaves

Put the yogurt into a square of muslin, tie it to a wooden spoon, then rest the spoon across the rim of a deep pan so that the bundle of yogurt is suspended within the pan. Leave for 1 hour to allow excess liquid to drain from the yogurt into the pan.

Light the barbecue. Once the coals are ready for cooking, brush the tomatoes with the oil and place them on the barbecue grill. Cook for 5–10 minutes until golden and roasted on the underside. Now turn the tomatoes over and cook for another 5 minutes until golden and roasted all over. (Alternatively, cook the tomatoes in a hot frying pan until golden.)

Remove the yogurt from the muslin, add half the salt and chilli powder and mix well. Spread the spiced yogurt on a serving plate, then arrange the roasted tomatoes on top. Sprinkle over the remaining salt and chilli powder and set aside.

To make the tadka, heat the ghee in a small pan and add the mustard seeds and curry leaves. Once the mixture begins to sizzle, pour it over the tomatoes and yogurt and serve.

Pavlova is a versatile dessert in that you can change the topping to use what's in season. I love making pavlovas in the summer with different fruits, but for this recipe, I am skipping fruit altogether! This pavlova is topped with some cream and beautifully caramelized walnuts, then drizzled with dark chocolate ganache – the perfect crunchy pudding to follow a lovely barbecue.

Caramelized walnut and coffee pavlova

SERVES 8–10

FOR THE MERINGUE

2 teaspoons cornflour

2 teaspoons cider vinegar

2 tablespoons instant coffee granules

1 teaspoon vanilla extract

6 egg whites

300g (10½oz) caster sugar

Preheat the oven to 120°C (250°F), Gas Mark ½. Draw a circle with a diameter of 25cm (10in) on a sheet of baking paper, then place this paper on a baking sheet.

Place the cornflour, vinegar, coffee and vanilla in a small bowl and stir to dissolve the coffee. Set aside.

Whisk the egg whites in a spotlessly clean mixing bowl until they form soft peaks. Now slowly add the sugar, 1 tablespoon at a time, whisking continuously. Once the sugar is incorporated, whisk for a further minute until the mixture is glossy and stiff. Now add the reserved coffee mixture and whisk for a few seconds.

Spread the mixture in a circle on the prepared baking sheet, using your drawn circle to guide you. Shape the mixture to resemble a crater, with the sides a little taller than the centre. Bake for 1½ hours until the meringue is crispy and dried out. Set it aside to cool completely. (You can make the meringue a couple of days in advance of serving and store it in an airtight container once cooled.)

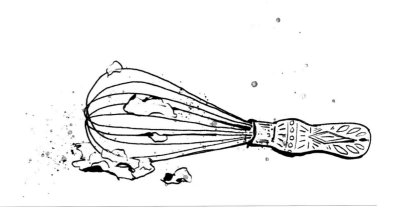

FOR THE CARAMELIZED WALNUTS

120g (4¼oz) walnuts

50g (1¾oz) caster sugar

20g (¾oz) unsalted butter

FOR THE GANACHE

100g (3½oz) dark chocolate, roughly chopped

200ml (7fl oz) double cream

FOR THE TOPPING

500ml (18fl oz) double cream

2 tablespoons caster sugar

Meanwhile, prepare the caramelized walnuts. Put the walnuts, sugar and butter into a pan and cook over a low heat for 6–8 minutes until the sugar turns to caramel. Transfer the nuts to a sheet of baking paper immediately and separate them while they are still hot. Set aside to cool, then chop them up roughly.

To make the ganache, first place the chopped chocolate in a heatproof bowl. Now heat the cream in a saucepan over a low heat until it is just about to boil. Pour the hot cream into the bowl of chocolate and stir until the chocolate has melted. Set aside to cool.

Make the topping when you are ready to serve. Put the cream and sugar into a bowl and whip until the mixture forms soft peaks.

To assemble the pavlova, place the meringue on a serving plate, top with the whipped cream, then drizzle over the chocolate ganache. Sprinkle the caramelized walnuts on top and serve immediately.

See photograph overleaf.

Just thinking about the flavour of this drink makes my mouth tingle! Being both sweet and salty, this Indian lemonade is extremely satisfying, and wonderfully light and refreshing on a hot summer's day.

Skikanji

SERVES 4

¼ teaspoon cumin seeds

6–8 mint leaves, plus extra mint sprigs to decorate

4 glasses of water

4 tablespoons caster sugar

¼ teaspoon kala namak (black salt)

pinch of freshly ground black pepper

8 tablespoons lemon juice

ice cubes, to serve

Toast the cumin seeds in a hot pan for 2 minutes until they begin to change colour. Using a pestle and mortar, crush them to a coarse powder. Now add the mint leaves to the mortar and crush them with the ground cumin to blend them together.

Put the measured water into a jug. Add the sugar, salt and pepper and stir until the sugar has dissolved. Now add the lemon juice and the crushed mint and cumin and mix well. Taste the drink and adjust the seasoning as desired. Add some ice and decorate with mint sprigs to serve.

I have very fond memories of picnics growing up in India. My aunt, who we called Guddo Maasi, had a farm just outside the town where we lived. During school holidays, my mum, aunts, cousins and I would pile into the back of their farm truck and go to the farm for lunch. I remember that, in the winters, Guddo Maasi's family would grow chickpeas, and we would pick the green ones to munch on. The grown-ups would pack the best picnic and we would demolish it while sitting on haystacks. The recipes I have selected for this chapter are a lovely mix of snacks and larger dishes. If you want a more snack-based picnic, go for the Bread Pakora Squares, Paneer Samosas or the Chutney Club Sandwich. The Veg Cutlet is delicious. It can be enjoyed on its own or served in buns for a bigger meal, accompanied by the Chickpea Salad. If you are planning a longer day out and want a substantial meal, then the Red Chilli Pulao with Chicken or the Paneer and Egg Chapati Rolls are your best bet. These meals are filling, delicious and great for sharing if you have a big group to feed. You can, of course, prepare the whole menu and take it all with you! The Mango Panna is deliciously refreshing, and the Coffee and Walnut Cake with Cardamom is a real crowd-pleaser.

Picnic

Veg cutlet

Chickpea salad

Chutney club sandwich

Bread pakora squares

Paneer and egg chapati rolls

Red chilli pulao with chicken

Paneer samosas

Courgette chutney

Mango chutney

Coffee and walnut cake with cardamom

Mango panna

Every time I visit my parents in India, we go to a specific coffee house that serves all sorts of Indian food, from dosa to biryani, and everything tastes delicious. Their veg cutlets are particularly popular. Made with a mixture of vegetables and coated in breadcrumbs, these are just so tasty, and provide the inspiration for this recipe. My veg cutlets are lovely hot or at room temperature, and are great for picnics and packed lunches. Serve them with just some chutney or in a burger bun for a more substantial meal.

Veg cutlet

MAKES 8

3 medium potatoes, peeled and cut into 1-cm (½-in) pieces

1 carrot, peeled and cut into 1-cm (½-in) pieces

1 beetroot, peeled and cut into 1-cm (½-in) pieces

10 green beans, cut into 1-cm (½-in) pieces

¼ teaspoon salt

¼ teaspoon chilli powder

¼ teaspoon ground cumin

6 tablespoons cornflour

80g (2¾oz) dried breadcrumbs

sunflower oil, for frying

Put the prepared vegetables into a saucepan and cover them with water. Bring the water to the boil, then boil for 10–12 minutes until cooked through and soft. Drain the vegetables and set aside to cool for a few minutes.

Using a potato masher, mash the vegetable medley. Now add the salt and spices, then the cornflour, and mix well. Divide the mixture into 8 equal portions. Shape each portion into a small ball, then squash it slightly with the palm of your hand.

Put the dried breadcrumbs on a plate, then press the squashed veg balls into the breadcrumbs to coat them on each side.

Heat the oil in a frying pan over a medium heat. Add the veg balls and cook for 1 minute on each side until beautifully golden. Using a slotted spoon, transfer to a plate lined with kitchen paper to drain briefly. Serve immediately, or leave to cool before packing into an airtight container for your picnic or packed lunch.

A few leaves in a bowl are just not for me!
I like salads with bite and body to them, and
this one has tons of both with the addition
of spiced-up chickpeas. The chaat masala
adds heat as well as sourness to light up the
chickpeas, and the refreshing dressing binds
all the elements together in a delicious salad.

Chickpea salad

SERVES 4

2 tablespoons rapeseed oil

1 teaspoon cumin seeds

1 green chilli, finely chopped

½ teaspoon salt

2 teaspoons chaat masala

2 × 400g (14oz) cans of
chickpeas, drained and rinsed

1 cucumber, roughly chopped

1 red onion, roughly chopped

1 Little Gem lettuce, roughly
chopped

FOR THE DRESSING

3 tablespoons extra-virgin
olive oil

2 tablespoons lemon juice

10–12 mint leaves, finely
chopped

pinch of salt

pinch of freshly ground
black pepper

Heat the oil in a saucepan over a medium heat, then
add the cumin seeds and the green chilli. Let them
sizzle for a few seconds and then reduce the heat to
low. Mix in the salt and chaat masala, followed by the
chickpeas. Cook over a high heat for 5 minutes until
the chickpeas are slightly crispy. Transfer them to a
serving bowl and leave to cool to room temperature.

Once the chickpeas have cooled, add the cucumber,
onion and lettuce to the bowl.

Put the dressing ingredients into a small bowl and
whisk to combine. Pour the dressing over the salad,
toss well and serve immediately, or pack into a
container to take on your picnic.

This stunner is inspired by the most famous Indian sandwich – the Bombay sandwich – which comprises layers of veggies combined with a lovely coriander chutney. I also draw inspiration from another favourite, the club sandwich, to make this version. For an insanely flavourful filling I use both courgette and mango chutneys, and introduce some cheese for added depth. If you prefer, you can use coriander chutney (see page 54) for a more traditional flavour.

Chutney club sandwich

MAKES 2

2 tablespoons salted butter for frying, plus extra, softened, for spreading

6 slices of white bread

Courgette Chutney (see page 157), to taste

1 medium potato, boiled, peeled and thinly sliced

1 tomato, thinly sliced

½ cucumber, thinly sliced

1 beetroot, boiled, peeled and thinly sliced

½ teaspoon chaat masala

Mango Chutney (see page 159), to taste

4 slices of Cheddar cheese

Spread butter on 1 slice of bread, then spread courgette chutney over the butter. Arrange half the slices of potato, tomato, cucumber and beetroot over the slice, sprinkling a little chaat masala after every layer. Butter the second slice of bread, spread over the mango chutney, then position this slice over the vegetables with the buttered side facing up. Place 2 slices of cheese on top of the second slice of bread, then seal the sandwich with another slice of buttered bread, this time with the buttered side facing down. Repeat the process to build the second sandwich.

Heat 1 tablespoon butter in a frying pan over a medium heat. Once the butter has melted, carefully place 1 of the prepared sandwiches in the pan. Cook the sandwich for a couple of minutes on each side until crispy and golden. Press the sandwich while cooking to seal it well. Transfer to a plate, cook the second sandwich in the same way, then serve, or leave to cool slightly and pack for your picnic.

This popular street-food snack is also often made in Indian homes. There are many variations – filled, coated, dipped, shallow-fried or deep-fried, to name a few. I make them as small squares, which are ideal for taking on a picnic or in a packed lunch. The filling carries a big flavour load, while the batter seals the sandwich perfectly and gives it a great crisp texture. Enjoy these squares with my Mango Chutney (see page 159) or Courgette Chutney (see page 157), although my kids love them with some tomato ketchup.

Bread pakora squares

MAKES 16

8 slices of white bread, crusts removed

4 tablespoons Courgette Chutney (see page 157)

sunflower oil, for deep-frying

FOR THE FILLING

2 tablespoons sunflower oil

1 onion, finely chopped

½ teaspoon salt

½ teaspoon ground turmeric

½ teaspoon chilli powder

½ teaspoon amchur (mango powder)

2 medium potatoes, boiled, peeled and mashed

FOR THE BATTER

300g (10½oz) gram flour

350ml (12fl oz) water

1 teaspoon salt

1 teaspoon ground turmeric

1 teaspoon chilli powder

1 teaspoon carom seeds (ajwain)

First, make the filling. Heat the oil in a saucepan, then add the onion and cook over a medium heat for 5 minutes until softened. Stir in the salt and spices and cook for a few seconds, then add the cooked and mashed potatoes and mix well. Set aside to cool slightly, then divide the filling into 4 equal portions.

Combine the batter ingredients in a large bowl and mix well. The resulting batter should be a little thinner than pancake batter.

To prepare the sandwiches, place 4 slices of bread on your work surface, spread some chutney over each slice, then spread a portion of the potato mixture on top. Top with another slice of bread to close the sandwich. Now cut each sandwich into 4 equal squares.

Heat the oil in a deep saucepan or deep-fat fryer to a cooking temperature of 170–180°C (340–350°F). (Maintain this temperature range throughout cooking.) Dip each sandwich square into the batter, ensuring it is fully covered. Once the oil is at cooking temperature, carefully place a batch of the battered squares in the oil and deep-fry for 1 minute on each side until golden. Remove the fried squares from the oil with a slotted spoon and transfer to a plate lined with kitchen paper to drain while you fry subsequent batches. Serve immediately, or leave to cool, then pack up for a picnic.

Why settle for sandwiches when you can make these splendid rolls? Inspired by the famous kathi rolls from the streets of India, they're easy to make – egg, tomato, yogurt, paneer and crisp red onion come together beautifully in these flavour-packed chapatis. This is one dish you'll want to make again and again.

Paneer and egg chapati rolls

MAKES 4

4 eggs

sunflower oil, for cooking

Red Onion Salad (see page 124)

FOR THE CHAPATIS

150g (5½oz) plain flour, plus extra for dusting

½ teaspoon salt

2 teaspoons sunflower oil

approximately 6 tablespoons water

FOR THE PANEER

2 tablespoons sunflower oil

1 teaspoon cumin seeds

1 green chilli, finely chopped

1 onion, finely chopped

1-cm (½-in) piece of fresh root ginger, finely chopped

4 garlic cloves, finely chopped

First, make the chapati dough. Put the flour, salt and oil into a mixing bowl. Mixing with your hands, slowly add just enough of the measured water (or more, if necessary) to bring the mixture together to form a soft dough. Knead the dough on a clean work surface for 2 minutes until smooth, then put it back into the bowl, cover the bowl with a clean tea towel and leave the dough to rest for 15–20 minutes.

While the dough is resting, prepare the paneer. Heat the oil in a saucepan over a medium–low heat, then add the cumin seeds. Cook for a few seconds until they begin to sizzle, then add the chilli, followed by the onion. Cook over a medium–low heat for 5 minutes until the onion has softened.

Add the ginger and garlic to the pan, mix well and cook for 1 minute. Stir in the tomato purée and the ketchup and cook over a low heat for 5 minutes. Next, stir in the salt and spices. Take the pan off the heat and stir in the yogurt, then return the pan to the heat and continue to stir for a couple of minutes. Now add the paneer and combine well. Cook for a couple of minutes, then take the pan off the heat and set aside while you cook the chapatis.

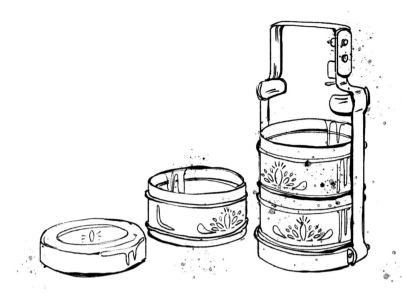

2 tablespoons tomato purée

2 tablespoons tomato ketchup

½ teaspoon salt

½ teaspoon ground cumin

½ teaspoon ground turmeric

½ teaspoon garam masala

3 tablespoons natural yogurt

225g (8oz) paneer, cut into rectangles

Divide the chapati dough into 4 equal portions. Roll out each portion on a lightly floured surface into a big circle with a diameter of 20–25cm (8–10in).

Heat a griddle pan and cook the first chapati over a medium–high heat for 1 minute on each side until it begins to change colour. While the chapati is cooking, whisk 1 egg in a bowl. Once the chapati is cooked on both sides, pour the beaten egg on top of the flatbread. Turn it over and drizzle 1 teaspoon oil around the edges of the chapati. Cook for 2 minutes until the egg is cooked, then turn over the chapati and drizzle another teaspoon of oil around the edges of the chapati. Cook for 1 minute, then transfer the cooked egg chapati to a plate. Cook the remaining chapatis in the same way.

Spoon a quarter of the paneer masala on the egg side of each chapati. Add some red onion salad on top. To roll, fold in 2 sides of the chapati, then roll up tightly. Cut each chapati in half to serve. Don't cut the rolls if you're taking them to a picnic – wrap them in kitchen foil and they're ready for transportation.

See photograph overleaf.

Pulao is one of the easiest ways to prepare rice and pack it with tons of flavour. This version is a spicy one, with a fiery chilli and garlic paste providing the most prominent flavour. If you are not a fan of too much chilli, skip the chilli-garlic paste part and just add chopped garlic and a little chilli powder to the pan when you cook the onion. But if you like your food a little hot, you are in for a treat! This dish is great served hot or at room temperature, making it an ideal filling meal for a picnic. You can make this rice dish with potatoes instead of chicken if you want to keep it vegetarian.

Red chilli pulao with chicken

SERVES 4

6 dried red chillies

6 garlic cloves

2 tablespoons water

2 tablespoons sunflower oil

1 teaspoon cumin seeds

1 large onion, thinly sliced

1½ teaspoons salt

1 teaspoon garam masala

¼ teaspoon freshly ground black pepper

6 boneless, skinless chicken thighs, cut in half

300g (10½oz) basmati rice, washed and drained

600ml (20fl oz) boiling water

Soak the dried chillies and garlic in some warm water for 15 minutes, then drain and, using a pestle and mortar, grind to a paste with the measured water.

Heat the oil in a saucepan over a medium–low heat, then add the cumin seeds and cook for a few seconds until they begin to sizzle. Stir in the onion and cook for 6–8 minutes until lightly golden. Add the chilli-garlic paste and cook over a low heat for 2 minutes to incorporate it. Now add the salt and spices and mix well, then stir in the chicken thighs. Increase the heat to high and cook for 5 minutes until slightly golden.

Next, add the rice to the pan and mix well. Now pour in the measured boiling water and bring it back to the boil. Cover the pan with a lid, reduce the heat to low and cook for 15 minutes until the rice is cooked and all the water has been absorbed. Let the pulao rest for 15 minutes before removing the lid to serve. If you're taking it on a picnic, pack it in a food container once it has cooled slightly and eat it the same day.

Samosas are one of my all-time favourite snacks and I particularly love the ones sold as street food. Over the years, I've shared many different samosa recipes. These are crispy on the outside, with a beautifully spiced paneer filling. Samosas are ideal picnic fare, or you could serve them as party canapés or with some salad as a starter. For me, they will always be the perfect snack to enjoy with some chutney.

Paneer samosas

MAKES 16

8 sheets of filo pastry

sunflower oil, for deep-frying

Courgette Chutney (see opposite) or Mango Chutney (see page 159), to serve

FOR THE FILLING

2 tablespoons sunflower oil

1 teaspoon mustard seeds

1 green chilli, finely chopped

1 onion, finely chopped

4 garlic cloves, finely chopped

½ teaspoon salt

½ teaspoon ground turmeric

½ teaspoon chilli powder

½ teaspoon garam masala

1 teaspoon chaat masala

100g (3½oz) frozen peas

225g (8oz) paneer, crumbled or cut into small pieces

FOR THE STICKY PASTE

2 tablespoons plain flour, plus extra for dusting

2 tablespoons water

To make the filling, heat the oil in a saucepan over a medium–low heat, then add the mustard seeds and cook for a few seconds until they begin to pop. Stir in the chilli and onion and cook for 5 minutes until they begin to soften.

Add the garlic to the mixture and cook for another minute. Next, mix in the salt and spices, followed by the peas. Cook for 5 minutes until the peas are soft. Add the paneer and mix well, then cook for a couple of minutes more. Take the pan off the heat and set aside to allow the filling to cool completely, then divide it into 16 equal portions.

For the sticky paste, blend the flour and measured water together in a bowl.

Cut the filo sheets in half lengthways. Place 1 long sheet of pastry on a lightly floured surface, and keep the others covered with a damp tea towel to prevent them from drying out.

To fold your first samosa, put 1 portion of the filling in a corner of the pastry, then fold the corner of the end of the pastry across the filling in a triangle. Keep folding the filled pastry over and over until you have used up the length of the pastry sheet. Seal the sides of the triangle by applying some of the sticky paste between the pastry edges, then pinching them together. Repeat the process with the remaining pastry sheets and filling to fold all the samosas.

Heat the oil in a deep saucepan or deep-fat fryer to a cooking temperature of 160–170°C (325–340°F). (Maintain this temperature range throughout cooking.) Carefully slide the filled pastries into the hot oil and cook for 1 minute on each side until golden and crispy. Using a slotted spoon, transfer the pastries to a plate lined with kitchen paper to drain. Serve hot or at room temperature with your choice of chutney.

I know courgette chutney might sound unusual, but once you try it, you'll understand how well the creaminess of courgettes marries with the other ingredients. It's so simple to prepare, you might well find yourself making this chutney all the time. Enjoy it with snacks, curries, breads... in fact, you'll find it enhances just about anything!

Courgette chutney

2 tablespoons rapeseed oil

1 teaspoon cumin seeds

6 garlic cloves, finely chopped

1 onion, finely chopped

1 courgette, finely chopped

handful of coriander leaves, finely chopped

¼ teaspoon salt

1 teaspoon soft light brown sugar

1 tablespoon lemon juice

FOR THE TADKA

1 tablespoon sunflower oil

1 teaspoon mustard seeds

1 teaspoon chilli flakes

Heat the oil in a saucepan over a medium–low heat and add the cumin seeds. Cook for a few seconds until the seeds begin to pop, then stir in the garlic and cook for 1 minute. Mix in the onion and cook for 5 minutes until it begins to soften.

Next, add the courgette, cover the pan with a lid and cook over a low heat for 6–8 minutes until the veg has softened. Add the coriander, salt, sugar and lemon juice and cook for 1 minute.

Transfer the mixture to the bowl of a blender and blitz it to a smooth consistency. Alternatively, use a pestle and mortar to create a slightly coarser chutney. Transfer it to a serving bowl.

To make the tadka, heat the oil in a small saucepan over a medium–low heat, then add the mustard seeds. Cook for a few seconds until they begin to sizzle, then stir in the chilli flakes and take the pan off the heat. Pour this tadka over the chutney and serve.

You can transport the chutney to your picnic spot in an airtight container, and store leftovers in the refrigerator for up to 2 days.

There are so many snacks this chutney works well with, and it's also great in sandwiches, salads and much more. I'm not the biggest fan of sweet chutneys – I like them with a bit of spice and a kick of chilli – so while this chutney certainly ticks the sweet box, it is vibrant and alive.

Mango chutney

2 tablespoons sunflower oil

1 teaspoon nigella seeds

4 garlic cloves, finely chopped

1-cm (½-in) piece of fresh root ginger, finely chopped

3 red chillies, finely chopped

½ teaspoon salt

¼ teaspoon ground turmeric

¼ teaspoon ground cinnamon

¼ teaspoon ground cardamom

¼ teaspoon ground cumin

¼ teaspoon ground coriander

2 large mangoes, peeled, stoned and cut into 1–2-cm (½–¾-in) pieces

150g (5½oz) caster sugar

3 tablespoons white vinegar

Heat the oil in a saucepan over a medium–low heat, then add the nigella seeds. Cook for a few seconds until they begin to sizzle, then stir in the garlic, ginger and chillies and let them cook for a few seconds. Now add the salt and spices, followed by the mangoes, and mix well, then stir in the sugar. Next, add the vinegar and mix well, then cover the pan with a lid and cook over a low heat for 50–60 minutes, stirring occasionally, until the mangoes have softened and the chutney has thickened. Leave to cool completely before serving.

Transport the chutney to your picnic spot in an airtight container, and store the leftovers in the refrigerator for up to 2 weeks.

Both my kids love this cake. Whenever we're heading out for a picnic, a day at the beach or a trip to the park, or if we're just having friends over for a chill afternoon, this is the dessert that Sia and Yuv will ask me to make. So, I decided it was high time the recipe made an appearance in one of my books. The cake is flavoured with coffee and cardamom, sandwiched and topped with a layer of fresh cream, decorated with walnuts, and is simply perfect!

Coffee and walnut cake with cardamom

SERVES 8–10

FOR THE CAKE

250g (9oz) unsalted butter, softened, plus extra for greasing

2 tablespoons instant coffee granules

4 tablespoons hot milk

250g (9oz) caster sugar

4 eggs

250g (9oz) plain flour

2 teaspoons baking powder

1½ teaspoons ground cardamom

50g (1¾oz) walnuts, roughly chopped

FOR THE FILLING AND TOPPING

200g (7oz) mascarpone cheese

50g (1¾oz) caster sugar

300ml (½ pint) double cream

50g (1¾oz) walnuts, roughly chopped

Preheat the oven to 180°C (350°F), Gas Mark 4. Grease and line 2 × 20cm (8in) round cake tins.

Dissolve the coffee granules in the hot milk in a small cup. Set aside.

Beat together the sugar and butter in a mixing bowl using a wooden spoon until pale and fluffy – you can use a stand mixer or electric whisk if you prefer. Add the eggs and whisk for a few seconds. Now add the flour, baking powder, cardamom and coffee milk and whisk until combined well. Next, fold in the walnuts.

Divide the batter equally between the prepared tins. Bake for 20–25 minutes until a skewer inserted into the centre of each cake comes out clean. Allow the cakes to cool in the tins for 5 minutes, then transfer to a cooling rack and set aside to cool completely.

To make the filling and topping, put the mascarpone and sugar into a bowl and beat together with a wooden spoon until smooth. Now add the cream and whisk until the mixture forms soft peaks.

Place 1 cake layer on a serving plate and spread with half the cream filling. Place the second cake layer carefully on top to sandwich the filling, then spread the remaining cream mixture on top and sprinkle with the walnuts.

In India, this is a popular drink to help beat the heat during the hot summers. It is made with small green mangoes that I find in Asian groceries during summer months. The sour, sharp flavour of these mangoes is very refreshing. If you can't get hold of them, try the really hard green mangoes you find in supermarkets – select the ones that look the most underripe. These will still make a lovely drink that tastes a little sweeter, so add the juice of a lemon for a sharper, more refreshing flavour.

Mango panna

SERVES 4

4 small green mangoes, peeled, stoned and cut into 1-cm (½-in) cubes (roughly 250g/9oz prepared weight)

100g (3½oz) caster sugar

300ml (½ pint) water

10–12 mint leaves, plus extra sprigs to decorate

1 teaspoon cumin seeds

1 teaspoon kala namak (black salt)

ice cubes, to serve

Put the mango cubes in a saucepan and add enough water to cover them (approximately 500ml/18fl oz). Bring the water to the boil over a high heat, then cook over a low heat for 1 hour until the mangoes are totally mushy and broken up. If the mango becomes too dry, add another 100ml (3½fl oz) water to the pan.

Put the sugar, measured water and mint into another pan and bring to the boil. Reduce the heat and simmer until the sugar has dissolved. Take the pan off the heat and set aside to cool completely, then strain to remove the mint leaves.

Using a potato masher, mash the mango, then pass it through a sieve. Stir the sieved mango into the cooled sugar syrup.

Heat a frying pan over a low heat and toast the cumin seeds for a couple of minutes until they are fragrant and begin to change colour. Crush the toasted seeds using a pestle and mortar, then mix the crushed cumin and salt thoroughly into the mango mixture.

Put ice into 4 glasses, pour the drink into the glasses and serve decorated with mint sprigs.

Festive food is something I miss about India. We celebrate so many festivals there, and each comes with its own specific dishes. I would need a lifetime to cover the foods of every Indian festival, so for this chapter, I'm sticking with Diwali, the Festival of Lights, as it is the biggest Hindu festival. I have so many stories about Diwali celebrations, each close to my heart. The streets and houses are decorated with lights, special oil *diyas* (lamps) are lit and there is colour everywhere. Beautiful *rangolis* (floor decorations) are carefully made with coloured powders, and flower garlands are hung from all the walls. And the food…oh, it is truly special! From snacks like Nimki or Gujiya to sweets such as Gulab Jamun, each is different in texture and flavour. I have some remarkable dishes lined up for your festive feast. Chickpea Curry, Tandoori Paneer Curry, Chilli-garlic Chicken and Peanut Aubergine Masala – there's something for everyone. All can be served with the amazing Masala Puri and Fenugreek Pea Pulao. If you're ever tempted to serve all of these dishes together, please do not hesitate! You will not be disappointed. All the effort you put in will make a meal to remember. But any dish you choose to cook from this chapter will be special on its own and make any celebration that little bit more memorable.

Festive feasts

Tandoori paneer curry

Nimki

Peanut aubergine masala

Chilli-garlic chicken

Chickpea curry

Fenugreek pea pulao

Poppy seed potatoes

Mint raita

Masala puri

Gulab jamun

Gujiya

By cooking paneer in tandoori masala with some yogurt and spices, you give it a delicious coating. When you then add the paneer to a tasty curry, you layer flavour upon flavour to make the ultimate dish for paneer-lovers. I have two of those at home – both my kids are big fans of paneer and they love this dish.

Tandoori paneer curry

SERVES 4

450g (1lb) paneer, cut into 2.5-cm (1-in) cubes

6 tablespoons sunflower oil

2 onions, finely chopped

2.5-cm (1-in) piece of fresh root ginger, finely chopped

4 garlic cloves, finely chopped

1 green chilli, finely chopped

400g (14oz) can of chopped tomatoes

100ml (3½fl oz) water

½ teaspoon salt

½ teaspoon ground turmeric

1 teaspoon chilli powder

1 teaspoon garam masala

1 teaspoon tandoori masala

3 tablespoons double cream

FOR THE MARINADE

150ml (¼ pint) natural yogurt

¼ teaspoon salt

½ teaspoon chilli powder

¼ teaspoon ground turmeric

1 teaspoon tandoori masala

Put all the marinade ingredients into a large bowl and mix well. Now add the paneer cubes and combine gently to ensure all the paneer pieces are coated well. Cover the bowl and leave to marinate for 30 minutes.

Heat 4 tablespoons of the oil in a saucepan over a medium–low heat. Add the paneer pieces without crowding them to ensure they cook evenly. Cook for 1 minute, then turn them over and cook for 1 minute more until golden. Leave the paneer to one side.

Heat the remaining oil in the same pan and add the onions. Cook these over a medium–low heat for 8–10 minutes until nicely golden.

Stir the ginger, garlic and green chilli into the onions in the pan and cook for 1 minute. Now mix in the canned tomatoes and measured water, cover the pan with a lid and cook over a low heat for 15 minutes.

Add the salt and spices to the pan, followed by the cooked paneer cubes. Combine well, then stir in the cream and serve immediately.

Sitting down with a cup of tea, you could easily plough through a batch of these seriously moreish pastry triangles before you'd even realized. As with other popular festival snacks, nimkis come in many variations. In our house, we would make one called namak para, which has fewer layers, and although that version is great, it is the extra layers in nimki (which become so wonderfully flaky when cooked with ghee) that make this a special version.

Nimki

MAKES 20

250g (9oz) plain flour, plus extra for dusting

½ teaspoon salt

½ teaspoon cumin seeds

½ teaspoon nigella seeds

½ teaspoon chilli powder

2 tablespoons ghee

100ml (3½fl oz) water

sunflower oil, for deep-frying

FOR THE PASTE

3 tablespoons plain flour

3 tablespoons ghee, melted

Put the flour, salt and spices into a bowl and mix well. Now add the ghee and rub it into the flour with your fingers until the mixture resembles breadcrumbs. Using your hands, slowly mix in the measured water until you have a soft dough. Knead the dough for a few seconds, then place it in the bowl, cover the bowl with a clean tea towel and set aside to rest for 30 minutes.

To make the paste, mix the flour and ghee together in a small bowl. Set aside.

Divide the dough into 2 equal portions. Roll out 1 portion on a lightly floured surface into a thin circle with a diameter of around 35cm (14in). Brush some of the paste over the dough circle, then roll up the dough tightly. Now cut it into 10 equal pieces.

Working with 1 piece at a time, press down gently to flatten the piece a little, then roll it into a rough square about

10–13cm (4–5in) across. Brush with some paste, then fold the square into a triangle by joining 2 opposite corners. Brush with more paste, then fold the other 2 corners to meet one another. Pierce the triangle all over with a fork.

Once you have completed rolling, folding and piercing all 10 pieces you cut from the first circle, repeat the process with the remaining half of the dough.

Heat the oil in a deep saucepan or deep-fat fryer to a cooking temperature of 150°C (300°F). (Maintain this temperature throughout cooking; if the oil is too hot, the outsides of the nimkis will turn golden, but they will not be cooked through.) Cook the pastry triangles in small batches for 2–3 minutes on each side until crispy and golden. Using a slotted spoon, transfer the nimkis to a plate lined with kitchen paper and leave to drain while you cook subsequent batches.

A nutty, spicy stuffing for baby aubergines, cooked in coconut milk, makes for a delicious curry to enjoy with some naan or rice. Try to source mini aubergines for this particular recipe. It's not possible to fill and fry large aubergines, and although you can still use those (cut into pieces instead of filled) for a similar flavour, the stuffed baby aubergines look spectacular – ideal for a festive table.

Peanut aubergine masala

SERVES 4

8 baby aubergines

rapeseed oil, for shallow-frying

2 onions, thinly sliced

6–8 fresh curry leaves

½ teaspoon salt

½ teaspoon ground turmeric

1 teaspoon garam masala

400ml (14fl oz) can of coconut milk

FOR THE FILLING

80g (2¾oz) blanched peanuts

2 tablespoons gram flour

1 teaspoon ground cumin

1 teaspoon chilli powder

1 teaspoon ground coriander

1 teaspoon ground turmeric

2 tablespoons tomato purée

2 tablespoons rapeseed oil

½ teaspoon salt

½ teaspoon honey

First, make the filling. Toast the peanuts in a pan over a low heat for 3–4 minutes until they turn golden. Then, using a pestle and mortar, crush them to a coarse powder.

Put the gram flour into the same pan and toast it over a low heat for 2 minutes until it begins to change colour. Once done, transfer the toasted gram flour to a mixing bowl, add the peanut powder and the remaining filling ingredients and mix well.

Cut a big, deep cross in the base of each baby aubergine, then fill these cuts with the peanut filling.

Heat the oil in a large frying pan over a medium heat. Carefully place the filled baby aubergines in the hot oil and fry for 5 minutes until golden, turning them over a couple of times. Transfer to a plate and set aside.

Remove all but 2 tablespoons of the oil from the pan. Add the onions and curry leaves and cook over a medium–low heat for 8–10 minutes until golden.

Mix the salt and spices into the onions in the pan, then stir in the coconut milk. Next, add the fried aubergines along with any leftover filling. Cover the pan with a lid and cook over a medium–low heat for 10 minutes. Turn over the aubergines, re-cover the pan with the lid and cook for another 5 minutes or until they are cooked through. Serve hot.

This curry is inspired by the popular Mangalorean chicken curry known as kori gassi. A friend made this curry for me once and I completely fell in love with it. In Mangalore they use the byadgi chillies, giving the dish its characteristic fiery colour. Relying on ingredients that are easily available to me, I've substituted Kashmiri chillies, which can be found in Indian groceries and even in many supermarkets. Also, instead of using fresh coconut milk, my version uses the canned stuff. If you are a fan of any of my chicken curries, I promise you will love this one. The flavour is to die for!

Chilli-garlic chicken

SERVES 4

3 tablespoons sunflower oil

12 shallots, cut into quarters

12 garlic cloves, peeled

12 dried Kashmiri chillies

2 tablespoons ghee

1 teaspoon fenugreek seeds

2 teaspoons cumin seeds

1 teaspoon black peppercorns

3 tablespoons coriander seeds

400ml (14fl oz) can of coconut milk

1 tablespoon tamarind paste

1½ teaspoons salt

1 teaspoon ground turmeric

5 skinless chicken thighs, plus 5 drumsticks (or use 1 whole chicken, cut into 10 skinless pieces on the bone)

FOR THE TADKA

2 tablespoons ghee

10 fresh curry leaves

1 cinnamon stick

Heat 2 tablespoons of the oil in a saucepan over a medium–low heat. Add the shallots and garlic and cook for 5–6 minutes until they soften. Using a slotted spoon, transfer these to a plate and set aside.

Pour the remaining oil into the same pan and add the chillies. Cook over a medium–low heat for 1 minute until they start to sizzle, then transfer them to the plate of shallots and garlic.

Now add the ghee to the same pan and throw in all the whole spices. Let them sizzle over a medium–low heat for 1 minute, then transfer the spice blend to the bowl of a blender with the reserved shallots, garlic and chillies and blitz the mixture to a smooth paste.

Transfer the paste back to the pan. Add the coconut milk, tamarind paste, salt and turmeric and mix well. Bring the mixture to the boil, then add the chicken pieces. Cover the pan with a lid and cook over a low heat for 45–50 minutes or until the chicken is cooked through.

To make the tadka, heat the ghee in a small saucepan over a medium–low heat, then add the curry leaves and cinnamon and cook until they begin to sizzle. Pour this tadka evenly over the chicken curry. You can serve the curry immediately, but I advise making it a couple of hours in advance to give the meat time to sit in the pan and soak up the flavours of all those spices, which makes it even more delicious. Simply reheat it gently before serving.

Popularly known as chole, this wonderful dish is enjoyed all year round in India and always appears on the dining table at festivals and weddings. There are many ways of making it – each family has their own recipe and this version is mine. If you have the time, allow the curry to sit for a couple of hours after cooking. Not only does this allow the flavours to infuse more intensely, it also enables the curry to thicken and emulsify a little, making the texture even better.

Chickpea curry

SERVES 4–6

400g (14oz) dried chickpeas

1.2 litres (2 pints) cold water

1 litre (1¾ pints) boiling water

2 black teabags

2 black cardamom pods

¼ teaspoon bicarbonate of soda

1 teaspoon salt

FOR THE MASALA

4 tablespoons sunflower oil

1 teaspoon cumin seeds

1 cinnamon stick

1 teaspoon carom seeds (ajwain)

2 onions, finely chopped

2.5-cm (1-in) piece of fresh root ginger, finely chopped

6 garlic cloves, finely chopped

Soak the chickpeas in a saucepan in the measured cold water overnight. Next morning, add the measured boiling water and teabags (which help to deepen the colour of the chickpeas), black cardamom, bicarbonate of soda and salt. Bring to the boil and cook over a medium heat for 1½ hours (or for longer if required) until the chickpeas are soft and cooked through.

To make the masala, heat the oil in a separate saucepan over a medium–low heat. Add the cumin seeds, cinnamon stick and carom seeds and allow them to sizzle for a few seconds, then mix in the onions. Cook over a medium–low heat for 8–10 minutes until the onions are deeply golden.

Mix the ginger, garlic and chilli into the saucepan and cook over a medium–low heat for another minute. Now add the tomatoes and measured boiling water, cover the pan with a lid and cook over a low heat for 25 minutes until the mixture is mushy and soft.

1 green chilli, finely chopped

2 tomatoes, finely chopped

200ml (7fl oz) boiling water

1 teaspoon ground turmeric

1 teaspoon chilli powder

2 teaspoons garam masala

handful of fresh coriander leaves, finely chopped

Next, add all the ground spices to the pan. Remove the teabags and black cardamom from the chickpeas, add the chickpeas along with any remaining liquid to the pan and stir well to combine. If the mixture is too dry, add another 100–200ml (3½–7fl oz) boiling water. Cover the pan with a lid and cook over a low heat for 1 hour until the curry has thickened and the chickpeas are super-soft.

To finish, use a potato masher to press the chickpeas no more than 3–4 times – you want to squash only a handful of the chickpeas to help thicken the sauce. Sprinkle over the coriander and serve immediately, or leave to rest before reheating and serving.

See photograph overleaf.

Fresh fenugreek (*methi*) leaves have a distinct flavour that I absolutely love. They are great as a sabji (vegetable dish), stuffed into flatbreads or in rice. Their slight bitterness goes really well with the sweetness of the peas in this wonderful dish. Fresh fenugreek leaves can be tricky to find, so I always get excited if I spot them in the grocers. It takes a bit of patience to pick the leaves from the stems, but this labour of love is worth it for special occasions.

Fenugreek pea pulao

SERVES 4–6

300g (10½oz) bunch of fresh fenugreek leaves

2 tablespoons sunflower oil

1 teaspoon cumin seeds

1 onion, thinly sliced

2.5-cm (1-in) piece of fresh root ginger, grated

100g (3½oz) frozen peas

1 teaspoon salt

1 teaspoon chilli powder

300g (10½oz) basmati rice, washed and drained

600ml (20fl oz) boiling water

Start by prepping the fenugreek leaves. Pick the leaves from the stems, then chop them up. Give the chopped leaves a good wash, then set them aside.

Heat the oil in a saucepan over a medium–low heat. Add the cumin seeds and cook for 1–2 minutes until they begin to sizzle. Now stir in the onion and cook for 5–6 minutes until softened.

Mix the ginger into the onion in the pan and cook over a medium–low heat for 1 minute, then stir in the frozen peas and cook for 4–5 minutes until they have softened.

Next, mix in the chopped fenugreek leaves, then cover the pan with a lid and cook over a medium–low heat for 2 minutes until they have wilted. Remove the lid and cook over a high heat for 2 minutes until any excess water has cooked off.

Now add the salt, chilli powder and rice and mix well. Pour in the measured boiling water, cover the pan with a lid and cook over a low heat for 15 minutes until the rice is cooked. Switch off the heat, then leave the rice to rest without lifting the lid for 15 minutes before serving.

This recipe is inspired by the Bengali dish alu posto, which is a very different potato curry to any you'll find elsewhere in India. In my version, two simple ingredients – potatoes and poppy seeds – come together so beautifully. The sum is truly greater than the parts.

Poppy seed potatoes

SERVES 4

40g (1½oz) white poppy seeds

180ml (6¼fl oz) water

3 green chillies

2 medium potatoes, peeled and cut into 2.5-cm (1-in) pieces

2 tablespoons rapeseed oil

2 bay leaves

½ teaspoon salt

½ teaspoon chilli powder

1 tablespoon lemon juice

Soak the white poppy seeds in 80ml (2¾fl oz) of the measured water for 1 hour. Using a pestle and mortar, grind the seeds with the soaking water and the chillies to form a paste.

Put the potato pieces into a saucepan, cover generously with water and bring to the boil, then cook the potatoes for 6–8 minutes until soft and cooked through. Drain and set aside.

Heat the oil in a saucepan over a medium–low heat. Add the bay leaves and cook for 1–2 minutes until they begin to sizzle. Add the poppy seed paste, then the remaining 100ml (3½fl oz) measured water. Now add the cooked potatoes, salt and chilli powder and mix well. Cover the pan with a lid and cook over a low heat for 5 minutes. To finish, add the lemon juice, mix well and serve immediately.

Yogurt in some shape or form will always be on the dinner table in Indian homes, and raita is a popular way of serving it. The mint and cucumber in this version are a classic combination, and pomegranate gives added crunch to this cooling dish and makes it extra special.

Mint raita

SERVES 4

200ml (7fl oz) natural yogurt

¼ teaspoon salt

¼ teaspoon freshly ground black pepper

½ teaspoon ground cumin

10 mint leaves, finely chopped

½ cucumber, grated

handful of fresh pomegranate seeds

Put the yogurt, salt, spices and mint into a bowl and mix well.

Squeeze out any excess liquid from the grated cucumber. Now add this to the bowl with the pomegranate seeds, mix well and serve.

Puri is a very popular type of bread in India and is often enjoyed at festivals, weddings and other special occasions. The dough is similar to chapati dough, but for this recipe I have added some lovely spices to it. The joy comes from deep-frying the dough until it puffs up. Puris are amazing served hot, but are often taken cold on picnics and train journeys in India to eat with some dry sabji (vegetable curry).

Masala puri

MAKES 20

300g (10½oz) chapati flour, plus extra for dusting

½ teaspoon salt

½ teaspoon chilli powder

½ teaspoon ground turmeric

1 teaspoon ground coriander

1 teaspoon carom seeds (ajwain)

approximately 220–240ml (7½–8½fl oz) water

sunflower oil, for deep-frying

Put the flour, salt and spices into a bowl and mix well. Now slowly add just enough of the measured water (or more, if necessary) to bring the mixture together into a soft dough. Knead the dough for 2 minutes, then leave the dough in the bowl, cover the bowl with a clean tea towel and set aside to rest for 15–30 minutes.

Divide the dough into 20 equal portions and shape these into small balls. Working on a lightly floured surface, roll them out into thin circles with a diameter of roughly 7.5cm (3in).

Heat the oil in a deep saucepan or deep-fat fryer to a cooking temperature of 170–180°C (340–350°F). (Maintain this temperature range throughout cooking.) Gently place 1 puri into the oil and let it puff up. After 1 minute, turn it over in the oil and cook for another minute. Using a slotted spoon, remove the puri from the oil and transfer it to a bowl. Cook the remaining puris one at a time in this way. Serve immediately.

Famous throughout the world, this popular Indian sweet always appears at festivals and is often served with *rabdi* (thickened sweetened milk) at weddings. Most Indian restaurants will have gulab jamun on the dessert menu, and they are even available canned in supermarkets! Delicate, fragrant and delicious, they are actually quite easy to prepare, so I highly recommend that you try making them at home.

Gulab jamun

MAKES 14

FOR THE SYRUP

300g (10½oz) granulated sugar

300ml (½ pint) water

1 teaspoon rosewater

6 cardamom pods, slightly crushed

FOR THE DOUGH

100g (3½oz) milk powder

40g (1½oz) plain flour

½ teaspoon baking powder

1 tablespoon ghee, plus about 300g (10½oz) for deep-frying

1 tablespoon natural yogurt

4 tablespoons milk

Put the syrup ingredients into a saucepan and bring to the boil. Reduce the heat so that the liquid simmers gently, then allow the mixture to bubble away until the sugar has melted. Take the pan off the heat and set aside.

While the sugar syrup is cooling, make the dough. Put the milk powder, flour and baking powder into a bowl and mix well. Now add the ghee and rub it into the flour mixture with your fingers to combine. Add the yogurt and milk and, using your hand, mix everything together to form a dough. It might be slightly stickier than chapati dough, but that's okay.

Heat the ghee in a deep saucepan or deep-fat fryer to a cooking temperature of 140°C (275°F). (Maintain this temperature throughout cooking.) Ensure the lukewarm pan of sugar syrup is at hand.

While the ghee is coming up to cooking temperature, divide the dough into 14 equal portions and roll them in your hands to form smooth balls. Once the ghee is at cooking temperature, carefully slide the dough balls, one at a time, into the ghee and cook for a couple of minutes until caramelly brown.

Using a slotted spoon, lift the jamun out of the hot ghee and put them directly into the lukewarm sugar syrup. Ensure the syrup is no hotter than lukewarm, otherwise the gulab jamuns will spread and dissolve. Leave them to soak in the syrup for 5 minutes, then serve warm.

If you are not serving the jamuns straight away, place them in an airtight container, sitting in some of the syrup, then store this in the refrigerator for up to 3–4 days. You can serve them chilled, but I prefer to warm them in the microwave for 10 seconds before serving.

These delicious little pockets are usually stuffed with dried fruits and nuts, and sometimes with *khoya* (thickened milk) or coconut – there are all sorts of variations. They appear at festivals not just on the dining table but are also given as edible gifts. I love them filled with *khoya*, but as I can't get hold of it where I live, and making it is a slow process, I depart from tradition and use nuts with ricotta cheese. This delicately tasty combo provides the perfect filling for these little treats. Enjoy them freshly cooked, warm or at room temperature.

Gujiya

MAKES 16

sunflower oil, for deep-frying

FOR THE PASTRY

3 tablespoons ghee

300g (10½oz) plain flour, plus extra for dusting

125ml (4fl oz) water

FOR THE FILLING

80g (2¾oz) almonds

80g (2¾oz) cashew nuts

60g (2¼oz) icing sugar, plus extra to decorate

½ teaspoon ground cardamom

120g (4¼oz) ricotta cheese

First, make the dough for the pastry. Rub the ghee into the flour in a mixing bowl until the mixture resembles breadcrumbs. Add the measured water a little at a time as you mix with your hand to form a soft dough. Knead the dough for a few seconds, then leave it in the bowl, cover the bowl with a clean tea towel and set aside to rest for 30 minutes

Meanwhile, make the filling. Put the almonds and cashew nuts into the bowl of a blender or mini-blender and blitz to a coarse powder. Transfer the powder to a mixing bowl, add the icing sugar and cardamom and mix well. Now add the ricotta and mix well.

Divide the dough into 16 equal portions. Working on a lightly floured surface, roll out each portion into a circle with a diameter of roughly 10cm (4in). Place approximately 1 tablespoon of the filling on one half of the circle, leaving the very edge of the filled semicircle clear. Using your finger, dab a little water along this clear edge, then fold the other half of the dough over the filling and press the edges together to seal well. Now make simple twists or folds around the edge (like a Cornish pasty or a gyoza) to decorate and consolidate the seal.

Heat the oil in a deep saucepan or deep-fat fryer to a cooking temperature of 150–160°C (300–325°F). (Maintain this temperature range throughout cooking.) Fry the gujiyas in batches for 2 minutes on each side until golden and crispy. Using a slotted spoon, transfer the gujiyas to a plate lined with kitchen paper and leave to drain while you cook subsequent batches. Serve once they have cooled down slightly, decorated with sifted icing sugar.

As my kids grow up, everyone in the family is so busy, with various school and work commitments and different activities. The respite offered on Sunday makes it such a treasured day, as it allows us all to be together, so Sunday meals are my favourite of the week. And that is why I like to make them special. Because everyone is slow to wake up on Sunday, we tend to sit down to brunch to enjoy a meal together and catch up. To make it an extra-special meal, Kacchi Biryani is my first choice. It takes a bit of time and effort, but it's worth it. Enjoy it with some Onion Raita or the Coconut-curry Leaf Chutney. If you want to add more dishes to the table, cook the Street-style Egg Curry and Parotha with it. You could also throw in the Spicy Semolina Vada for a crunchy snack. But if you want to keep things lazy on your Sunday morning, try the Cheesy Egg Toast or the Masala Vermicelli, both of which are simple dishes that pack a flavour punch. I have also added an easy Rava Dosa recipe for those who, like me, love South Indian food. This version needs no overnight soaking, and can be prepared last-minute and served with Hearty Wholesome Dal. My kids love the Chocolate and Cardamom Caramel Cake, so this often makes an appearance on Sundays. Give it a go – it might become your favourite, too!

Sunday brunch

Cheesy egg toast

Hearty wholesome dal

Parotha

Kacchi biryani

Street-style egg curry

Spicy semolina vada

Rava dosa

Onion raita

Coconut-curry leaf chutney

Masala vermicelli

Chocolate and cardamom caramel cake

Eggs are my favourite for Sunday mornings, and this is my upscaled egg dish for special weekend brunches. Inspired by the famous Mumbai dish eggs kejriwal, this cheesy toast has a layer of chutney for added flavour, then is topped with a perfectly fried egg for a wholesome and delicious start to your day of relaxing.

Cheesy egg toast

SERVES 4

100g (3½oz) Cheddar cheese, grated

1 green chilli, roughly chopped

handful of coriander leaves and stems, finely chopped

4 spring onions, finely chopped

4 slices of sourdough bread (or any bread of your choice)

4 tablespoons Coriander Yogurt Chutney (see page 54)

2 tablespoons olive oil

4 eggs

salt and freshly ground black pepper

chilli flakes, to garnish

Preheat the grill on a medium setting.

Combine the cheese, chilli, coriander and spring onions in a bowl and mash the ingredients up well by hand or using a fork. Set aside.

Toast the bread in a toaster or in a frying pan over a medium heat for 1 minute until lightly golden.

Spread 1 tablespoon chutney over one side of each slice of bread. Now spread the cheese mixture over this. Transfer the topped bread slices to a baking tray and grill for 3–4 minutes until the cheese has melted and turned golden.

Meanwhile, heat the oil in a frying pan over a medium heat. Break the eggs into the pan, cover the pan with a lid and cook for 3 minutes until the whites are cooked but the yolks are still runny. Place 1 fried egg on each slice of cheesy toast, sprinkle with salt and pepper and chilli flakes and serve immediately.

SERVES 4

FOR THE DAL

120g (4¼oz) chana dal
(split yellow peas)

200g (7oz) whole urad dal
(black lentils)

1 teaspoon salt

1 teaspoon ground turmeric

2.5-cm (1-in) piece of fresh
root ginger, grated

4 garlic cloves, grated

2 bay leaves

1 cinnamon stick

2 litres (3½ pints) boiling
water

FOR THE TADKA

2 tablespoons sunflower oil

2 tablespoons ghee

1 teaspoon cumin seeds

2 green chillies, finely
chopped

1 onion, roughly chopped

2.5-cm (1-in) piece of fresh
root ginger, finely chopped

4 garlic cloves, grated

1 tomato, finely chopped

½ teaspoon salt

½ teaspoon chilli powder

2 teaspoons ground
coriander

handful of coriander leaves,
finely chopped

200ml (7fl oz) boiling water

This dal is popularly known as ma chole ki dal. In Punjabi, black lentils (known as whole urad dal in Hindi) are called *ma ki dal*, and they make this dish creamy and hearty, while *chole* (also known as chana dal) make it thick and wholesome. This is crowd-pleasing comfort food for special occasions. All it needs is a bit of time and patience to allow it to cook gently and slowly.

Hearty wholesome dal

Put all the ingredients for the dal into a large saucepan and bring to the boil. Cook over a medium heat for 2 hours until the lentils are soft and cooked through.

Meanwhile, prepare the tadka. Heat the oil and ghee in a separate saucepan over a medium–low heat. Add the cumin seeds and let them sizzle for a few seconds, then stir in the chillies, onion, ginger and garlic and cook for 5–6 minutes until they begin to soften.

Stir in the tomato and cook for 5 minutes until soft. Now stir in the salt, spices and coriander, then the measured boiling water.

Now add the tadka to the cooked lentils and cook over a medium heat for 15 minutes until the dal has thickened slightly. Cover the saucepan and let the dal rest for 30 minutes to allow the flavours from the tadka to infuse the dal before serving.

These flatbreads are inspired by the famous Malabar parothas of Kerala. The dough is straightforward enough to make, but you do need to give it time to rest between the various steps, and you can't be stingy with the oil! This way, the dough relaxes, allowing the lovely flaky layers to appear. Indeed, it's these dreamy layers that make this special flatbread perfect for your Sunday feasts.

Parotha

MAKES 4

300g (10½oz) plain flour, plus extra for dusting

1 teaspoon salt

2 teaspoons caster sugar

100ml (3½fl oz) milk

approximately 150ml (¼ pint) sunflower oil

80ml (2¾fl oz) water

Mix together the dry ingredients in a large bowl. Stir in the milk and 1 tablespoon oil. Add the measured water a little at a time and, using your hand, bring the mixture together to form a soft dough. Knead for 5 minutes, then place the dough in the bowl, cover the bowl with a clean tea towel and set aside to rest for 30 minutes.

Divide the dough into 4 equal portions and shape them into balls. Drizzle 1 teaspoon oil over each dough ball to cover. Cover with the tea towel and leave to rest for 30 minutes.

Working with 1 dough ball at a time, roll out the ball on a lightly oiled work surface into a thin circle, then drizzle over 1 teaspoon oil and spread it over the dough circle. Using your fingers, stretch the dough into a circle with a diameter of 30–35cm (12–14in). Spread another teaspoon of oil over the circle, then pick up one side of the circle and fold it like a fan, pinching it together

until you have a long, gathered piece of dough. Twist this around your thumb to make a spiral (like a cinnamon roll), then tuck the tail of the dough into the centre of the spiral. Cover with the tea towel and leave to rest for 30 minutes.

Again working on 1 piece at a time, roll out the twisted dough ball into a circle with a diameter of roughly 20cm (8in).

Heat a frying pan to a high heat and, once hot, cook 1 parotha for 1 minute on each side. Now drizzle 1 teaspoon oil over the paratha and turn it over to cook that side again for 1 minute until golden. Meanwhile, drizzle 1 teaspoon oil over the surface now facing up. Once the underside is golden, flip the parotha and cook for another minute until both sides are golden. Transfer the cooked parotha to a clean surface and, using your hands, push the edges in towards the centre, encouraging the layers to open up. Repeat the process to cook the remaining parothas. Serve immediately.

Biryani is easily my death-row meal – that's how much I love it. I craved it when I was pregnant and would often stop at an Indian restaurant on my way home from work for a biriyani takeaway. Now I try out any new biryani recipe I find. This one belongs to my friend Sudhakar Mangam. It is his recipe for Hyderabad kacchi biryani. *Kacchi* means raw in Hindi, so instead of cooking the chicken first, then layering it into the rice, raw chicken and semi-cooked rice are cooked together in the oven. When the chicken is cooked *dum* (sealed) in this way, you get the most delicious flavours.

Kacchi biryani

SERVES 4–6

400ml (14fl oz) sunflower oil

4 onions, thinly sliced

1 whole chicken, skin removed, cut into approximately 14 pieces

FOR THE MARINADE

200ml (7fl oz) natural yogurt

1 teaspoon salt

1 teaspoon ground turmeric

1 teaspoon garam masala

2 teaspoons ground coriander

1 teaspoon ground cumin

1 cinnamon stick

6 cardamom pods

6 cloves

2 bay leaves

1 star anise

6 garlic cloves, grated

2.5-cm (1-in) piece of fresh root ginger, grated

2 green chillies, roughly chopped

handful of coriander leaves and stems, finely chopped

Heat the oil in a saucepan, then add the onions and cook over a medium heat for 15–18 minutes until golden. Transfer the onions to a sieve, set this over the pan you cooked them in and leave to drain. Once drained, divide the onions into 2 equal portions and set aside (or refrigerate 1 portion in an airtight container, if marinating the chicken overnight – see below). Also reserve 2 tablespoons of oil from the pan.

To make the marinade, put the yogurt, salt, ground spices, whole spices, garlic, ginger, chillies, fresh herbs, 1 portion of reserved fried onion and the reserved oil into a mixing bowl. Combine well, then add the chicken pieces. Mix well to coat the chicken, cover the bowl and leave in the refrigerator to marinate for a minimum of 1 hour or overnight if you have the time.

When ready to cook, preheat the oven to 220°C (425°F), Gas Mark 7. Put the measured boiling water into a large saucepan with the salt and whole spices and bring back to the boil. Add the rice and cook over a medium–low heat for 5 minutes until the edges of the rice grains begin to soften. It is important that the rice is only 25 per cent cooked at this point. Drain the rice, reserving the cooking water.

10–12 mint leaves, finely chopped

1 portion reserved fried onion (see method)

2 tablespoons reserved oil (see method)

TO COOK

2 litres (3½ pints) boiling water

1 teaspoon salt

1 star anise

6 cloves

6 black peppercorns

2 bay leaves

4 cardamom pods

350g (12oz) basmati rice, washed and drained

2 tablespoons milk

pinch of saffron threads

2 tablespoons sunflower oil

2 teaspoons kewra water

4 tablespoons ghee

1 portion reserved fried onion (see method)

Put the milk and saffron into a small saucepan and heat over a high heat for 1 minute (alternatively, heat in the microwave for 40 seconds). Leave to one side for 5 minutes to infuse.

Heat the oil in a heatproof casserole dish, then add the chicken pieces with all the marinade and cook over a high heat for 5 minutes until the meat begins to colour.

Spread the semi-cooked rice on top of the chicken, then pour 150ml (¼ pint) of the reserved rice cooking water on top. Drizzle the kewra water and the saffron milk all over the rice. Now spoon the ghee all around the rice. Cover the casserole with the lid and bake the biryani for 50 minutes. Remove the dish from the oven and let it sit for 15 minutes before removing the lid. Don't be tempted to lift the lid during this time, or you will lose the steam, which continues to cook the dish during the resting time. Once the resting time has elapsed, check that the chicken is cooked through (see page 119) before serving.

Sprinkle over the second portion of reserved fried onion to serve.

See photograph overleaf.

FOR THE EGGS

8 eggs

pinch of salt

pinch of chilli powder

pinch of ground turmeric

4 tablespoons sunflower oil

FOR THE CURRY

1 tablespoon sunflower oil

2 tablespoons salted butter

1 teaspoon cumin seeds

2 onions, finely chopped

4 garlic cloves, finely chopped

2.5-cm (1-in) piece of fresh root ginger, finely chopped

2 green chillies, 1 finely chopped, 1 thinly sliced

70g (2½oz) tomato purée

400ml (14fl oz) boiling water

½ teaspoon salt

½ teaspoon ground turmeric

1 teaspoon chilli powder

1 teaspoon garam masala

2 teaspoons ground coriander

1 teaspoon caster sugar

150ml (¼ pint) natural yogurt

2 tablespoons double cream

Egg curries are often found in *dhabas* (roadside cafes) and small restaurants, served with the proper tandoori roti made in hot fiery tandoor ovens. Yet I can't help but associate Sunday mornings at home with egg curry, served with piping-hot home-made parothas (see page 198), and all the family feasting together. This is such a simple dish to make, yet it's luxurious and rich, and so very comforting.

Street-style egg curry

Boil the eggs for 8 minutes. Drain, then stand them under cold running water to cool. Once cooled, peel the eggs. Cut each of the peeled eggs in half and sprinkle the egg halves with the salt, chilli powder and turmeric.

Heat the oil in a frying pan. Cook the eggs over a medium heat for 1 minute on each side until golden. Set aside while you make the curry.

Heat the oil and butter in a saucepan. Add the cumin seeds and cook over a medium–low heat until they begin to sizzle. Now stir in the onions, garlic, ginger and the finely chopped chilli and cook for 8–10 minutes until the onions are deep golden.

Stir the tomato purée and half the measured boiling water into the saucepan, then cover the pan with a lid and cook over a low heat for 15 minutes until thickened.

Add the salt, spices and sugar to the pan, mix well and cook for 1 minute. Now take the pan off the heat, add the yogurt and the remaining measured water and stir for a minute. Return the pan to the hob and cook over a low heat for 5 minutes to allow the spices to infuse the yogurt. Add the cream and stir it through. Now place the reserved eggs on top, sprinkle over the thinly sliced chilli and serve.

These are dangerous! I would happily eat my way through a whole batch of them piled up on my plate, all by myself. They are super-crispy on the outsides and tender and scrumptious on the insides, full of herby goodness, with crunch from the onion, warmth from the cumin and a tangy sourness from the mango powder. Utterly irresistible! Enjoy them with any chutney you like, but I highly recommend the Coriander Yogurt Chutney (see page 54) or the Chana Dal Chutney (see page 85) with these.

Spicy semolina vada

MAKES ABOUT 24

200g (7oz) semolina

50g (1¾oz) self-raising flour

½ teaspoon salt

½ teaspoon chilli powder

300ml (½ pint) natural yogurt

1 onion, finely chopped

1 green chilli, finely chopped

handful of coriander leaves, finely chopped

10–12 mint leaves, finely chopped

8 fresh curry leaves, finely chopped

1 teaspoon ground cumin

1 teaspoon amchur (mango powder)

sunflower oil, for cooking

Mix the semolina, flour, salt and chilli powder in a bowl. Now add the yogurt and mix well. Cover the bowl and leave to rest for 30 minutes.

After the resting time has elapsed, add the remaining ingredients, except for the oil, to the bowl and mix to combine.

Heat the oil in a deep saucepan or deep-fat fryer to a cooking temperature of 170–180°C (340–350°F). (Maintain this temperature range throughout cooking.) Take walnut-size portions of the mixture and carefully lower them into the oil. Cook over a medium heat for 5–6 minutes, turning the vadas over from time to time, until golden and crispy. Using a slotted spoon, transfer the vadas to a plate lined with kitchen paper to drain.

This light and crispy type of dosa, made with *rava* (semolina), is quick to make compared with normal dosa, for which you need a few days for fermenting the rice and lentils. Rava dosas provide the perfect quick meal that still feels like a huge treat. Serve them with a bowl of dal or some coconut chutney for a feast with delicious South Indian flavours.

Rava dosa

MAKES 4

120g (4¼oz) semolina

120g (4¼oz) rice flour

60g (2¼oz) plain flour

1 teaspoon salt

½ teaspoon chilli powder

1 teaspoon cumin seeds

¼ teaspoon freshly ground black pepper

1 red onion, finely chopped

2.5-cm (1-in) piece of fresh root ginger, finely chopped

10 fresh curry leaves, finely chopped

handful of coriander leaves and stems, finely chopped

1 tablespoon natural yogurt

900ml (1½ pints) water

sunflower oil, for cooking

Put all the ingredients, except the water and oil, into a large bowl and mix well. Now add half the measured water and whisk until smooth. Add the remaining water and whisk again. Cover the bowl and set the mixture aside to rest for 30 minutes.

Heat a frying pan until it is smoking hot. Put a few drops of oil in the pan, then wipe them away with a sheet of kitchen paper so that the pan is clean. Now ladle in the batter in a large circle, adding just enough to create a thin layer with some holes in it. These are characteristic of rava dosa, so don't fill them up with more batter. Drizzle 1 teaspoon oil all around the edges of the dosa and cook over a medium heat for roughly 2 minutes until the dosa is golden and crispy. Fold in half and serve immediately. Continue cooking the rest of the dosa batter in the same way.

Herby, crunchy and refreshing, this raita goes well with any meal. Feel free to add some cucumber, tomatoes or boiled potatoes if you want it to have more body, but I feel it's the simplicity of this raita that makes it so amazing.

Onion raita

SERVES 4

200ml (7fl oz) natural yogurt

1 red onion, finely chopped

½ teaspoon ground cumin

½ teaspoon kala namak
(black salt)

½ teaspoon chilli flakes

handful of coriander leaves
and stems, finely chopped

10–12 mint leaves, finely
chopped

Mix all the ingredients together in a bowl and serve. Store any leftover raita in an airtight container in the refrigerator for up to 2 days.

I love the rounded flavour of this super-simple, deliciously creamy chutney. The warming ginger, sour tamarind, spicy chilli and nutty dal, finished off with fragrant curry leaves, make it an exciting little dip.

Coconut-curry leaf chutney

2 tablespoons chana dal (split yellow peas)

flesh from ½ fresh coconut, roughly chopped

2 green chillies

2.5-cm (1-in) piece of fresh root ginger

1 teaspoon tamarind paste

½ teaspoon salt

16 fresh curry leaves

100ml (3½fl oz) water

FOR THE TADKA

2 tablespoons sunflower oil

1 teaspoon mustard seeds

1 tablespoon urad dal (split black lentils)

1 green chilli, thinly sliced

6 fresh curry leaves

Toast the chana dal in a frying pan over a medium–low heat for 3–4 minutes until lightly golden.

Transfer the toasted dal to the bowl of a blender and add the remaining ingredients. Blitz until the mixture is smooth, then transfer the chutney to a serving dish.

To make the tadka, heat the oil in a saucepan over a medium–low heat, then add the mustard seeds and urad dal. Cook for 1–2 minutes until they begin to sizzle, then add the chilli and curry leaves and cook for a few more seconds. Now pour this tadka over the chutney and serve immediately.

Known as seviyan, this dish is a favourite for Sunday breakfast or brunch and is often enjoyed with a nice cup of tea. It is easy to make and you can add any vegetables you might have in the refrigerator. Serve it on its own or with your favourite chutney. The key is to prepare it fresh – it's okay to cook the veg beforehand, but add the seviyan only when you're ready to eat.

Masala vermicelli

SERVES 4

200g (7oz) seviyan (fine vermicelli)

2 tablespoons sunflower oil

1 tablespoon salted butter

1 teaspoon cumin seeds

10 fresh curry leaves

1 onion, finely chopped

1 green chilli, roughly chopped

1 potato, peeled and roughly chopped

1 carrot, peeled and roughly chopped

1 red pepper, cored, deseeded and roughly chopped

100g (3½oz) frozen peas

¾ teaspoon salt

1 teaspoon chilli powder

½ teaspoon ground turmeric

1 teaspoon garam masala

1 teaspoon ground coriander

1 teaspoon chaat masala

200ml (7fl oz) boiling water

4 tablespoons lemon juice

Put the seviyan into a wide frying pan or saucepan and toast over a low heat for 3–4 minutes until it changes colour. Transfer the toasted seviyan to a bowl and set aside.

Heat the oil and butter in a saucepan. Add the cumin seeds and, once they begin to sizzle, add the curry leaves, onion and green chilli. Cook for 2 minutes until they begin to soften. Next, mix in the potato and carrot, cover the pan with a lid and cook over a low heat for 5 minutes until softened.

Add the pepper and peas to the pan and mix well, then cover the pan with the lid and cook over a low heat for another 2 minutes until they begin to soften. Now add the toasted seviyan, salt and spices and mix well. Next, stir in the measured water, then cover the pan again and cook for 8 minutes until all the water has been absorbed.

Take the pan off the heat and leave it to rest for 5 minutes before removing the lid. Then drizzle the lemon juice on top of the mixture and serve hot.

FOR THE SPONGE LAYERS

150ml (¼ pint) boiling water

1 tablespoon instant coffee granules

100ml (3½fl oz) sour cream

200g (7oz) unsalted butter, softened, plus extra for greasing

150g (5½oz) caster sugar

2 large eggs

1 teaspoon vanilla paste

150g (5½oz) plain flour

50g (1¾oz) cocoa powder

50g (1¾oz) ground almonds

½ teaspoon bicarbonate of soda

1 teaspoon baking powder

FOR THE GANACHE

250g (9oz) dark chocolate, roughly chopped

400ml (14fl oz) double cream

FOR THE CARAMEL

200g (7oz) caster sugar

220ml (7¾fl oz) double cream

1 teaspoon ground cardamom

Dry, flavourless cakes are so disappointing. This delightful sponge is moist and light, almost fudge-like when sandwiched with the dark chocolate ganache, and the cardamom-flavoured caramel adds just the right amount of sweetness to balance all the dark chocolate. If you want a luxurious ending to a special meal, this stunning triple-layered cake is always a winner.

Chocolate and cardamom caramel cake

First, make the sponge layers. Preheat the oven to 180°C (350°F), Gas Mark 4. Grease and line 3 × 20cm (8in) round cake tins. Put the measured boiling water, coffee and sour cream into a bowl or jug and mix well. Set aside.

Beat together the sugar and butter in a mixing bowl using a wooden spoon for roughly 2 minutes until smooth and pale – you can use a stand mixer or electric whisk if you prefer. Now gradually add the eggs and whisk until they are fully incorporated. Next, mix in the vanilla paste. Set aside.

Combine the dry ingredients in a separate mixing bowl and mix well.

Now add half the dry ingredients to the creamed butter-and-sugar mixture, followed by half the coffee-sour cream mixture. Using a balloon whisk or a stand mixer, mix until fully combined. Now add the remaining dry ingredients and coffee-sour cream mixture to the bowl and incorporate in the same way.

Divide the batter equally between the prepared cake tins. Bake for 15–20 minutes until a skewer inserted into the centres of the cakes comes out clean. Set aside to allow the cakes to cool completely in the tins.

While the sponge layers are cooling, prepare the ganache and caramel, starting with the ganache. First, place the chocolate pieces in a heatproof bowl. Now heat the cream in a pan over a low heat until it is almost at boiling point. Then pour the hot cream over the chocolate and leave to sit for 1 minute to allow the chocolate to begin melting. Now stir until all the chocolate has melted. Set aside to cool.

To make the caramel, heat the sugar in a saucepan over a low heat, stirring frequently, until it melts and becomes caramel. Now pour in the cream in a slow, steady stream and stir through. Mix in the ground cardamom, let the mixture bubble for 1 minute, then take the pan off the heat and set aside to allow the caramel to cool completely. Transfer the cooled caramel to a piping bag and snip off the tip.

To assemble the cake, first place 1 sponge layer on a serving plate. Spread one-third of the ganache over this, then pipe over one-third of the caramel. Align the second sponge layer on top, then repeat with the ganache and caramel. Top with the final cake layer, then spread the final portion of ganache on top and drizzle over the remaining caramel.

This cake is best served as soon as it is assembled. If you need to store it before serving, cover the cake and store it in the refrigerator. Remove it from the refrigerator 1 hour before serving to bring it up to room temperature.

See photograph overleaf.

Glossary of UK/US terms

UK	US
aubergine	eggplant
baking paper	parchment paper
baking tin	baking pan
baking tray	baking sheet
barbecue/barbecuing	grill/grilling
beetroot	beet
bicarbonate of soda	baking soda
biscuit	cookie
caster sugar	superfine sugar
chickpeas	garbanzo beans
chilli flakes	red pepper flakes
cider vinegar	apple cider vinegar
cocoa powder	unsweetened cocoa powder
coriander (fresh)	cilantro
cornflour	cornstarch
courgette	zucchini
crisps	potato chips
desiccated coconut	unsweetened desiccated coconut (or substitute unsweetened shredded)
double cream	heavy cream
filo pastry	phyllo dough
frying pan	skillet
gram flour	chickpea flour
grill	broil/broiler
groundnut oil	peanut oil
hob	stove
ice lolly	popsicle
icing sugar	confectioners' sugar
king prawns	jumbo shrimp
kitchen foil	aluminum foil
kitchen paper	paper towels
muslin	cheesecloth
passata	strained tomatoes
plain flour	all-purpose flour
rapeseed oil	canola oil
red/green pepper	red/green bell pepper
self-raising flour	self-rising flour
shop	store
sieve	strainer
spatchcock	butterfly
spring onions	scallions
starter	appetizer
stick blender	immersion blender
sultanas	golden raisins
takeaway	takeout
tea towel	dish towel
tomato purée	tomato paste

Index

Acknowledgements

Big thanks to my commissioner, Publishing Director Eleanor Maxfield, for her years of love and support. This is my seventh book with Eleanor and it has been such a joy and pleasure to work with her on every book. I am so grateful for the confidence and trust she has shown in me, and the way she allows me to go with my creative flow.

Thanks to the amazing team behind the book: Art Director Juliette Norsworthy, who spends so much time understanding the theme and getting it perfect every time; Senior Editor Leanne Bryan, who picks up things I have missed with her eagle eye and makes the text fit perfectly; and Production Manager Caroline Alberti, who works tirelessly behind the scenes to ensure the finished book looks as beautiful as it possibly can.

Thank you to the very talented Nassima Rothacker, who has photographed every single book of mine. She pours so much love and care into each photograph, bringing the food to life in the way only she can.

Thanks also to Food Stylist Rosie Reynolds, who understood my recipes instantly and cooked them with so much love and expertise. And thanks to Salima Hirani for her expert editing.

Big thanks to the whole team at Octopus for all your hard work.

And most importantly, thanks to my family – my husband Gaurav and kids Sia and Yuv – who really are the people living the book with me by eating all the food that features in it for months. They are so amazing when I am in the book-writing bubble. I could not do it without their immense love and support.